TypeScript for Web Development

Boost Your Productivity, Eliminate Costly
Errors, and Build Scalable Web
Applications with TypeScript

Adrian Miller

1

DISCLAIMER 5

INTRODUCTION 6

CHAPTER 1: INTRODUCTION TO TYPESCRIPT FOR WEB
DEVELOPMENT.. 9

THE POWER OF TYPESCRIPT FOR WEB DEVELOPMENT 12
SETTING UP TYPESCRIPT: INSTALLATION, CONFIGURATION, AND TOOLING 17

CHAPTER 2: TYPESCRIPT FUNDAMENTALS....................................... 23

UNDERSTANDING TYPESCRIPT'S TYPE SYSTEM: PRIMITIVES, OBJECTS, AND ENUMS
.... 29
WORKING WITH INTERFACES, TYPE ALIASES, AND UNION TYPES......................... 35

CHAPTER 3: ADVANCED TYPESCRIPT FEATURES........................... 42

MASTERING GENERICS FOR REUSABLE AND SCALABLE CODE 47
EXPLORING MODULES AND NAMESPACES FOR CODE ORGANIZATION 53

CHAPTER 4: TYPESCRIPT AND JAVASCRIPT INTEROPERABILITY
.... 59

USING TYPESCRIPT WITH JAVASCRIPT: GRADUAL ADOPTION STRATEGIES.......... 64
WORKING WITH THIRD-PARTY JAVASCRIPT LIBRARIES IN TYPESCRIPT............... 69

CHAPTER 5: TYPESCRIPT FOR THE DOM AND WEB APIS 74

STRONGLY-TYPED DOM MANIPULATION AND EVENT HANDLING........................ 78
USING FETCH API AND WORKING WITH JSON IN TYPESCRIPT............................ 83

CHAPTER 6: ASYNCHRONOUS PROGRAMMING WITH
TYPESCRIPT 89

MASTERING PROMISES, ASYNC/AWAIT, AND ERROR HANDLING 94
LEVERAGING TYPESCRIPT WITH RXJS FOR REACTIVE PROGRAMMING................. 99

CHAPTER 7: BEST PRACTICES FOR SCALABLE TYPESCRIPT
APPLICATIONS 106

WRITING MAINTAINABLE AND READABLE TYPESCRIPT CODE........................... 111
ENFORCING BEST PRACTICES WITH LINTERS, FORMATTERS, AND TSLINT/ESLINT
.... 117

CHAPTER 8: DEBUGGING AND TESTING TYPESCRIPT CODE.... 123

DEBUGGING TYPESCRIPT WITH SOURCE MAPS AND IDE TOOLS........................ 128
WRITING UNIT AND INTEGRATION TESTS WITH JEST AND CYPRESS 133

CHAPTER 9: TYPESCRIPT WITH REACT: STRONGLY-TYPED COMPONENTS.. 140

USING TYPESCRIPT WITH REACT: PROPS, STATE, AND HOOKS 147
ADVANCED REACT PATTERNS WITH TYPESCRIPT: CONTEXT API AND HOCS 155

CHAPTER 10: TYPESCRIPT WITH ANGULAR.................................... 161

LEVERAGING TYPESCRIPT IN ANGULAR APPLICATIONS...................................... 168
DEPENDENCY INJECTION AND STRONGLY-TYPED SERVICES 174

CHAPTER 11: TYPESCRIPT IN FULL-STACK WEB DEVELOPMENT
.... 180

SHARING TYPES BETWEEN FRONTEND AND BACKEND FOR CONSISTENCY 186
GRAPHQL WITH TYPESCRIPT: END-TO-END TYPE SAFETY................................. 192

CONCLUSION... 198

DISCLAIMER.. ERRO! INDICADOR NÃO DEFINIDO.

GLOSSARY: TYPESCRIPT FOR WEB DEVELOPMENT.................... 201

Disclaimer

The information provided in *"TypeScript for Web Development: Boost Your Productivity, Eliminate Costly Errors, and Build Scalable Web Applications with TypeScript"* by **Adrian Miller** is for educational and informational purposes only.

This Book is designed to provide insights into TypeScript programming and its applications in blockchain and Web3 development.

Introduction

In a time when web development is consistently advancing, the need for robust, scalable, and maintainable applications has reached unprecedented levels. As developers, our goal is to craft solutions that not only fulfill user requirements but also endure over time. Enter TypeScript—a powerful superset of JavaScript that has swiftly gained popularity within the development community for its capacity to enhance productivity while reducing the likelihood of errors.

"TypeScript for Web Development: Enhance Your Productivity, Reduce Costly Mistakes, and Create Scalable Web Applications with TypeScript" serves as your all-encompassing resource for unlocking the full capabilities of TypeScript in your web endeavors. Whether you are a seasoned JavaScript developer or a newcomer to the field, this eBook is designed to equip you with the knowledge and skills necessary to thrive in today's dynamic development environment.

Within these pages, you will uncover how TypeScript's static typing, sophisticated tooling, and contemporary features can transform your development workflow. We will examine how to smoothly incorporate TypeScript into existing JavaScript projects, allowing you to take advantage of type safety and enhanced code quality without the need to start anew. Furthermore, this guide will offer practical examples, best practices, and real-world applications, ensuring that you can implement your newfound knowledge right away.

You will discover how TypeScript aids in identifying errors at compile time, ultimately decreasing the time and expenses related to debugging and refactoring. As you gain expertise in TypeScript, you will find that it not only increases your productivity but also cultivates a more organized codebase, facilitating collaboration with team members and the onboarding of new developers.In this eBook, we will cover:

Introduction to TypeScript: Understand the fundamentals and key features that differentiate TypeScript from JavaScript.

Setting Up Your Environment: Get step-by-step guidance on installing TypeScript and configuring your development environment.

Type Annotations and Interfaces: Dive deep into static typing, learn how to define types, and discover the power of interfaces for creating structured code.

Advanced TypeScript Features: Explore generics, unions, and intersection types that will allow you to write flexible and reusable code.

TypeScript with Popular Frameworks: Learn how to integrate TypeScript with popular frameworks like React, Angular, and Node.js to enhance your development workflow.

Best Practices: Discover the best practices for writing clean, maintainable, and scalable code using TypeScript.

Real-World Projects: Apply your learned skills in hands-on projects that simulate real-world scenarios.

By the end of this eBook, you will not only be equipped with the technical knowledge necessary to implement TypeScript in your projects but also the confidence to explore advanced web development techniques. The future of web development is TypeScript, and with this guide, you are well on your way to becoming a more effective and innovative developer.

So, whether you're building your first app or looking to elevate your existing projects, let's embark on this exciting journey to mastering TypeScript together!

Chapter 1: Introduction to TypeScript for Web Development

TypeScript has emerged as a significant language in the field of web development. Created by Microsoft, TypeScript serves as a superset of JavaScript, incorporating static typing and additional features that enhance the robustness of the development process.

The introduction of TypeScript was aimed at addressing common challenges encountered with JavaScript, particularly in large-scale applications. Its creators sought to offer developers a more organized development experience while retaining the dynamic characteristics that JavaScript is celebrated for. As a result, TypeScript maintains a familiar syntax while integrating types, interfaces, and other sophisticated features, making it an attractive option for web developers.

Reasons to Utilize TypeScript

1. Static Typing

A key benefit of TypeScript is its static typing capability. This feature allows developers to define data types for variables, function parameters, and return values. By identifying type-related errors during the compilation process instead of at runtime, TypeScript reduces the chances of unforeseen bugs reaching production. This enhancement contributes to greater reliability, particularly in extensive applications where error tracing can be challenging.### 2. Enhanced IDE Support

Modern Integrated Development Environments (IDEs) and text editors can leverage TypeScript's rich type information to provide enhanced tooling support.

Features like autocompletion, type checking, and inline documentation become more powerful and intuitive with TypeScript. Developers can navigate their codebases with ease and receive informative feedback, which drastically enhances productivity.

3. Object-Oriented Programming Features

TypeScript adopts many of the principles of object-oriented programming (OOP), including classes, interfaces, and inheritance. These features empower developers to structure their applications in a more organized manner, making code easier to read, maintain, and scale. OOP concepts can help in creating modular code, which can be particularly beneficial when working in larger teams or on extended projects.

4. Seamless Integration with JavaScript

Since TypeScript is a superset of JavaScript, existing JavaScript code is valid TypeScript code. This allows developers to gradually adopt TypeScript in their projects without needing to rewrite everything from scratch. The evolution from JavaScript to TypeScript can be seamless, enabling teams to experience the benefits of typing while still using well-established JavaScript libraries and frameworks.

Getting Started with TypeScript

Before diving into the intricacies of TypeScript, it's important first to ensure that you have the development environment ready. The following steps will guide you through setting up TypeScript for your web development projects.

Step 1: Installation

To begin using TypeScript, you'll need to install it. The easiest way to do this is by using npm, the package manager for Node.js. If you haven't already installed Node.js, you can download it from the official website.

Once Node.js is ready, open your command line interface and run the following command:

```sh
npm install -g typescript
```

This command installs TypeScript globally on your system, making it accessible from any directory. ### Step 2: Creating a TypeScript Configuration File

After installation, you can initialize a new TypeScript project by creating a configuration file. This is done using the following command:

```sh
tsc --init
```

This will create a `tsconfig.json` file in your project directory. This file is crucial as it allows you to specify compiler options, file inclusion/exclusion, and more. By default, TypeScript will compile all `.ts` files in the directory, but these settings can be customized according to your project needs.

Step 3: Writing Your First TypeScript File

Start by creating a simple TypeScript file named `app.ts`. Inside this file, you can write some basic code:

```typescript
function greet(name: string): string { return `Hello,
${name}!`;
}

const message = greet("World"); console.log(message);
```

In this example, the function `greet` takes a parameter
`name` of type `string` and returns a greeting. This
shows how TypeScript's type annotations provide clarity
and help prevent type-related errors.

Step 4: Compiling TypeScript to JavaScript

To compile your TypeScript code into JavaScript, you can
run the TypeScript compiler (tsc) from the command line:

```sh
tsc app.ts
```

This command will generate an `app.js` file containing
the compiled JavaScript code. You can now execute this
JavaScript file in your browser or Node.js environment.

With its increasing popularity in the development
community, mastering TypeScript can be an invaluable
asset in your toolkit as a modern web developer.

The Power of typeScript for Web Development

Enter TypeScript—a statically typed superset of JavaScript

that is revolutionizing the way developers build web applications. This chapter delves into the power of TypeScript, exploring its advantages, key features, and how it enhances the web development experience.

Understanding TypeScript

TypeScript is an open-source language developed by Microsoft that extends JavaScript by adding static types. It compiles down to plain JavaScript, ensuring that it runs on any browser, server, or host that supports JavaScript. The primary goal of TypeScript is to improve the development process by introducing type- checking at compile time, thereby catching errors before the code is executed.

Static Typing: A Safety Net for Developers

One of the standout features of TypeScript is its static typing system. JavaScript's dynamic nature allows for great flexibility but often leads to bugs that can emerge at runtime. TypeScript mitigates this by enforcing type constraints, reducing the likelihood of runtime errors. Developers can define types for variables, function parameters, and return values, resulting in code that is more predictable and easier to debug.

For example, consider the following TypeScript function that adds two numbers:

```typescript
function add(a: number, b: number): number { return a + b;
}
```

By specifying that both parameters `a` and `b` must be numbers, and that the function returns a number, TypeScript ensures that any incorrect usage, such as passing a string, will be caught at compile time, alerting developers before deployment.

Enhanced Code Readability and Maintainability

TypeScript's type annotations and interfaces contribute significantly to code readability. A well-typed codebase is much easier to understand at a glance compared to JavaScript code that lacks type information. This readability is essential in large codebases where multiple developers work collaboratively.

Using interfaces, TypeScript allows developers to define the shape of objects clearly:

```typescript
```typescript interface User {

id: number; name: string; email: string;

}

const user: User = { id: 1,

name: 'Alice',

email: 'alice@example.com'

};
```
```

This declarative approach means developers can quickly grasp the data structure being utilized, reducing onboarding times for new team members and simplifying code reviews.

Tooling and IDE Support

TypeScript's design philosophy emphasizes developer experience, which is evident in its exceptional tooling and IDE support. Modern code editors like Visual Studio Code, WebStorm, and others provide powerful integrations that leverage TypeScript's type system to offer autocompletion, type checking, and inline documentation.

This enhanced development environment boosts productivity significantly. Developers can write code faster and with fewer errors, relying on their IDE to provide guidance and suggestions based on static types.

Refactoring becomes more straightforward, as the IDE can comprehensively analyze the type relationships in the code.

Adoption and Ecosystem Support

Since its introduction, TypeScript has seen widespread adoption among major frameworks and libraries. Frameworks like Angular, React, and Vue.js have built-in support for TypeScript, allowing developers to leverage its features while building modern web applications. TypeScript has also gained traction in the JavaScript community at large, with many libraries providing type definitions through DefinitelyTyped, making it easy for developers to use TypeScript with existing JavaScript libraries.

The increasing popularity of TypeScript means that many resources are available for learning and troubleshooting, including documentation, community forums, and courses. This broad support further strengthens its position as a powerful tool in the web developer's toolkit.

TypeScript in Action

To illustrate the power of TypeScript in web development, let's consider a practical example using a simple web application. Imagine a task management app where users can create and manage tasks.

Using TypeScript, we can define our data models, services, and components more robustly:

```typescript
interface Task {
id: number; title: string;
completed: boolean;
}
class TaskService {
private tasks: Task[] = [];
addTask(task: Task): void { this.tasks.push(task);
}
getTasks(): Task[] { return this.tasks;
}
}
```

In a real-world scenario, this structured approach helps organize the codebase, ensures type safety, and creates a clear contract for how tasks are handled within the application. It also aids in maintaining the application as it scales, making it easier to add new features or modify existing ones without introducing bugs.

The power of TypeScript in web development cannot be

overstated. Its static typing, enhanced readability, and exceptional tooling support provide developers with the resources they need to build robust, maintainable, and scalable applications. As the web continues to evolve, embracing TypeScript allows developers to stay ahead of the curve, fostering a development culture that values quality and efficiency.

Setting Up TypeScript: Installation, Configuration, and Tooling

TypeScript, a superset of JavaScript developed by Microsoft, has emerged as a powerful option, offering static typing, modern features, and elaborate tooling support. In this chapter, we'll explore how to set up TypeScript from installation to configuration and the essential tools that enhance your development experience.

1. Why TypeScript?

Before delving into the setup process, it's crucial to understand the benefits of TypeScript:

Static Typing: TypeScript allows you to define variable types, enabling catch errors during development rather than at runtime. This leads to more robust applications.

Enhanced IDE Support: With type definitions, editors can provide improved autocompletion, inline documentation, and refactoring tools.

Modern JavaScript Features: TypeScript supports the latest JavaScript features, making it compatible with ES6 and beyond while providing backward compatibility.

Large Ecosystem: Given its popularity, TypeScript is widely adopted in the industry, with many libraries and frameworks offering type support.

2. Installing TypeScript

Setting up TypeScript is a straightforward process. You can install it globally on your machine as well as locally within your project. The following instructions will guide you through both methods using Node.js and npm (Node Package Manager).

Install TypeScript Globally

Ensure Node.js is Installed: TypeScript requires Node.js. You can download it from nodejs.org.

Open Command Prompt or Terminal: Depending on your operating system, open the command line interface.

Install TypeScript:

Run the following command to install TypeScript globally:

```bash
npm install -g typescript
```

Verify the Installation: To ensure TypeScript is installed correctly, check the version:

```bash tsc -v
```

A successful output indicates that TypeScript has been installed properly. ### Install TypeScript Locally

For project-specific configurations, you'll often want to install TypeScript locally:

Create and Navigate to a New Project:

```bash
mkdir my-typescript-project cd my-typescript-project
```

Initialize a New npm Project:

This will create a `package.json` file:

```bash npm init -y
```

Install TypeScript Locally:

Execute the following command:

```bash
npm install --save-dev typescript
```

3. Configuring TypeScript

TypeScript uses a configuration file called `tsconfig.json` to define the settings and behavior of the compiler. Let's create this file and discuss its key options.

Create tsconfig.json:

In the project root directory, run:

```bash
npx tsc --init
```

Basic tsconfig.json File:

After running the initialization command, a `tsconfig.json` file will be created. Here's a simple configuration and explanations of key properties:

```json
{

"compilerOptions": { "target": "es6", "module": "commonjs", "strict": true, "esModuleInterop": true, "skipLibCheck": true,

"forceConsistentCasingInFileNames": true

},

"include": ["src/**/*"],

"exclude": ["node_modules", "**/*.spec.ts"]

}
```

compilerOptions: This section includes critical settings:

target: Specifies the JavaScript language version. Setting it to `es6` means your TypeScript will be compiled down to ES6 JavaScript.

module: Defines the module system to be used. `commonjs` is typical for Node.js projects.

strict: This enables all strict type-checking options.

esModuleInterop: This allows a seamless handling of JavaScript ES modules.

skipLibCheck: Skips type checking of declaration files

(`.d.ts`) for faster builds.

forceConsistentCasingInFileNames: Ensures file names are treated case-sensitive.

include: Specifies which files the TypeScript compiler should include. Here, it includes all TypeScript files in the `src` folder.

exclude: Specifies files and folders that should be ignored during compilation, usually the

`node_modules` and test files.

Compiling TypeScript:

Once the `tsconfig.json` file is set up, you can compile TypeScript files by running:

```bash
npx tsc
```

This command looks for the `tsconfig.json` file and compiles the TypeScript code based on the settings defined within it.

4. Tooling and Development Environment

To take full advantage of TypeScript, integrating additional tooling into your development workflow is paramount. Here are some essential tools and libraries for a smooth TypeScript experience:

Visual Studio Code: This feature-rich editor has first-class TypeScript support out of the box, making it easy to work with TypeScript's features like IntelliSense, code navigation, and error highlighting.

Type Definitions: For third-party libraries, you might

need to install type definitions. The [DefinitelyTyped](https://github.com/DefinitelyTyped/DefinitelyTyped) repository provides type definitions for most popular libraries, and you can install them using:

```bash

npm install --save-dev @types/library-name

```

Prettier: This code formatter integrates seamlessly with TypeScript, allowing you to format your code consistently.

ESLint: For maintaining code quality and consistency, ESLint can be set up with TypeScript support using the `@typescript-eslint` plugin.

Testing Frameworks: Consider using Jest or Mocha with TypeScript support, coupled with their respective type definitions, to ensure your code is reliable and bug-free.

Setting up TypeScript is a vital first step toward enhancing your JavaScript applications with static typing and more robust tooling. By installing TypeScript globally or locally, configuring the `tsconfig.json` file effectively, and leveraging essential tools such as IDEs, formatters, and testing frameworks, you place yourself in a stronger position to build maintainable and error-resistant applications.

Chapter 2: TypeScript Fundamentals

By understanding these core principles, you'll be better equipped to leverage TypeScript's capabilities in your projects. Let's dive in.

2.1 Introduction to TypeScript

TypeScript is a superset of JavaScript that compiles down to plain JavaScript. This means that any JavaScript code is also valid TypeScript code. TypeScript was developed by Microsoft and aims to address the limitations of JavaScript, especially when it comes to large-scale application development. The primary feature that sets TypeScript apart is its optional static type system, allowing developers to catch errors early in the development cycle and improve code quality.

2.1.1 Why Use TypeScript?

Several advantages make TypeScript an appealing choice for developers:

Static Typing: TypeScript allows developers to specify the types of variables, function parameters, and return values. This can help catch errors at compile-time rather than run-time, reducing debugging time.

Improved IDE Support: Many modern IDEs provide enhanced code completion, navigation, and refactoring tools when using TypeScript. This helps increase developer productivity.

Interoperability with JavaScript: As a superset of JavaScript, TypeScript allows you to gradually adopt the language within existing JavaScript projects. You can convert files from .js to .ts smoothly, which promotes easy integration.

Object-Oriented Features: TypeScript embraces object-oriented programming features, such as interfaces, inheritance, and access modifiers, making it easier to structure large applications.

2.2 Types in TypeScript

One of the cornerstones of TypeScript is its static type system. Types can be primitive, like numbers and strings, or complex, like arrays and objects. Understanding these types is crucial for effective TypeScript development.

2.2.1 Primitive Types

TypeScript has several built-in primitive types:

Number: Represents both integer and floating-point values.

```typescript
let age: number = 30;
```

String: Denotes textual data.

```typescript
let name: string = "Alice";
```

Boolean: Represents a truthy or falsy value.

```typescript
let isStudent: boolean = true;
```

2.2.2 Complex Types

Apart from primitive types, TypeScript facilitates the construction of complex types:

Arrays: Arrays can be declared with specific types.

```typescript
let scores: number[] = [90, 85, 92];
```

Tuples: Tuples allow you to express an array with a fixed number of elements with specific types.

```typescript
let person: [string, number] = ["Bob", 25];
```

Objects: You can define the shape of an object by creating an interface or declaring types inline.

```typescript interface Person {
name: string; age: number;
}
let employee: Person = { name: "Eve", age: 28 };
```

2.3 Functions and Type Annotations

Functions in TypeScript can be annotated with types to ensure that parameters and return values conform to the specified types.

2.3.1 Function Types

You can define the types of function parameters and return types:

```typescript
function add(x: number, y: number): number { return x + y;
}
```

2.3.2 Optional and Default Parameters

TypeScript allows you to mark parameters as optional using the `?` operator and to specify default values.

```typescript
function greet(name: string, greeting: string = "Hello"): string { return `${greeting}, ${name}!`;
}
```

2.4 Interfaces and Type Aliases

In TypeScript, interfaces and type aliases enable you to define custom types and enhance the structure of your code.

2.4.1 Interfaces

Interfaces define a contract in your code by specifying the

structure an object should adhere to.

```typescript
interface Car {
make: string; model: string; year: number;
}
```

2.4.2 Type Aliases

Type aliases allow you to create a new name for a type. This can be useful for more complex types.

```typescript
type StringArray = string[];
let names: StringArray = ["John", "Jane", "Doe"];
```

2.5 Classes and Inheritance

TypeScript supports modern class-based object-oriented programming, allowing you to create classes and utilize inheritance.

2.5.1 Defining Classes

Classes can include properties, methods, and constructors:

```typescript
class Animal {
constructor(public name: string) {}
speak(): void {
console.log(`${this.name} makes a noise.`);
}
}
```

```
```

2.5.2 Inheritance

You can extend classes using the `extends` keyword and override methods:

```typescript
class Dog extends Animal { speak(): void {

console.log(`${this.name} barks.`);

}

}
```

2.6 Advanced TypeScript Features

Beyond the basics, TypeScript provides advanced features that can greatly enhance your codebase.

2.6.1 Generics

Generics allow you to create functions, classes, or interfaces that can work with any data type while still enforcing type safety.

```typescript
function identity<T>(arg: T): T { return arg;

}
```

2.6.2 Enums

Enums are a special data type that allows you to define a set of named constants.

```typescript enum Direction {
```

Up, Down, Left, Right,

}

` ` `

2.6.3 Type Guards

Type guards are a way to determine the type of an object at runtime, enhancing TypeScript's type-checking capabilities.

` ` `typescript

function isString(test: any): test is string { return typeof test === "string";

}

` ` `

By leveraging these features, developers can build robust, scalable, and maintainable applications. As we progress through this book, we will dive deeper into TypeScript's advanced features and practical applications in real-world projects. Understanding the fundamentals is the first step to becoming proficient in TypeScript, and we hope you feel empowered to explore further.

Understanding TypeScript's Type System: Primitives, Objects, and Enums

This chapter aims to provide a comprehensive understanding of TypeScript's type system, focusing on three fundamental components: primitives, objects, and enums.

1. Primitives

In TypeScript, primitive types are the most basic data types that represent a single value. These types are foundational to most programming constructs and include:

1.1 Number

The `number` type represents both integer and floating-point numbers. In TypeScript, numbers are not differentiated between these forms, allowing for seamless mathematical operations.

```typescript
let age: number = 30;

let price: number = 19.99;
```

1.2 String

The `string` type is used for representing a sequence of characters. TypeScript allows you to define strings using single quotes, double quotes, or backticks (for template literals).

```typescript
let greeting: string = "Hello, World!";

let userName: string = `Hello, ${greeting}`;
```

1.3 Boolean

The `boolean` type allows you to use logical values, specifically `true` or `false`. This is particularly useful in conditional statements and logical operations.

```typescript
let isActive: boolean = true;

let isComplete: boolean = false;
```

1.4 Null and Undefined

TypeScript provides two special types: `null` and `undefined`. `null` is a value that represents an absence of a value, while `undefined` indicates that a variable has been declared but has not yet been assigned a value.

```typescript
let someValue: null = null;

let notAssigned: undefined = undefined;
```

1.5 Symbol

The `symbol` type is used to create unique identifiers for object properties. While less commonly used in everyday programming, it's essential for advanced JavaScript features.

```typescript
const uniqueId: symbol = Symbol('id');
```

1.6 BigInt

Introduced in ECMAScript 2020, the `BigInt` type allows for representation of integers larger than the maximum allowed `Number` value. This is particularly useful in applications that require high precision with large integers.

```typescript
let bigNum: BigInt = BigInt(1234567890123456789012345678901234567890);
```

2. Objects

In TypeScript, objects are more complex data structures that can encapsulate multiple values and functionalities. They can represent both mutable data structures and more complex, user-defined types.

2.1 Object Type

The `object` type in TypeScript can represent any non-primitive type. This includes arrays, functions, and collections.

```typescript
let user: object = { name: "Alice", age: 25, isActive: true

};
```

2.2 Interfaces

Interfaces form a critical part of TypeScript's type system. They enable you to define the shape of an object, which can then be implemented by classes or other objects.

```typescript
interface User {

name: string; age: number;

isActive: boolean;
```

32

```
}
let user1: User = { name: "Bob", age: 30, isActive: false
};
```
` ` `

2.3 Classes

TypeScript enhances JavaScript's class-based approach by introducing type annotations and access modifiers. Classes can be used to create reusable components that encapsulate both data and behavior.

` ` `typescript class Person {

```
constructor(public name: string, public age: number) {}

greet() {
return `Hello, my name is ${this.name} and I am ${this.age} years old.`;
}
}
let person1 = new Person("Charlie", 35);
```
` ` `

2.4 Arrays

Arrays in TypeScript can hold a collection of items of a specific type, ensuring predictable behavior and preventing errors during runtime.

` ` `typescript

```
let scores: number[] = [90, 85, 76, 88];
```

```
let items: Array<string> = ['apple', 'banana', 'orange'];
```

3. Enums

Enums are a powerful feature of TypeScript, allowing developers to define a set of named constants. Enums improve code readability and maintainability by providing meaningful names for numeric and string values.

3.1 Numeric Enums

Numeric enums automatically assign the first member a value of 0 and increment subsequent members by 1.

```typescript
enum Directions {
Up, Down, Left, Right
}
let move: Directions = Directions.Up;
```

3.2 String Enums

String enums, introduced to provide better semantic clarity, can be assigned string values, enhancing readability and debuggability.

```typescript
enum LogLevel {
Info = "INFO", Warn = "WARN",
Error = "ERROR"
}
let currentLogLevel: LogLevel = LogLevel.Error;
```

3.3 Heterogeneous Enums

Although less common, TypeScript allows for heterogeneous enums, which contain both string and numeric values, providing flexibility in certain scenarios.

```typescript
enum Mixed {
No = 0,
Yes = "YES",
}
```

The type system mitigates many common programming errors, making TypeScript not just a superset of JavaScript but a more powerful and expressive way to build applications.

Working with Interfaces, Type Aliases, and Union Types

This chapter will delve deep into three powerful features of TypeScript that are particularly beneficial for modern web development: Interfaces, Type Aliases, and Union Types. Understanding these constructs not only enables developers to create more robust and maintainable code but also improves the overall development experience through better tooling and error handling.

1. Interfaces

What are Interfaces?

Interfaces in TypeScript serve as a contract for classes and objects. They define the shape of an object, specifying what properties and methods an object should have. This adds a layer of abstraction and promotes the use of clean and modular code.

Creating Interfaces

To create an interface, you use the `interface` keyword followed by the name of the interface and its structure. Here's a simple example:

```typescript
interface User {
id: number; name: string; email: string;
}
```

In this example, the `User` interface describes an object that must have three properties: `id`, `name`, and `email`.

Implementing Interfaces

Classes can implement interfaces to ensure that they adhere to the specified structure. Here's how it works:

```typescript
class Admin implements User { id: number;
name: string; email: string;
constructor(id: number, name: string, email: string) {
this.id = id;
this.name = name; this.email = email;
}
displayUser(): void {
```

```
console.log(`ID: ${this.id}, Name: ${this.name}, Email:
${this.email}`);
}
}
```
```

In this example, the `Admin` class implements the `User`
interface, guaranteeing that it contains the required
properties and can use the defined methods.

### Extending Interfaces

Interfaces can also extend one another, allowing for a
more versatile design. For instance, if we want to create a
`Moderator` interface that builds on `User`, we can do so
as follows:

```typescript
interface Moderator extends User { permissions: string[];
}
```

Now, the `Moderator` interface includes all properties
from the `User` interface and adds a new property:

`permissions`.

Summary of Interfaces

Interfaces enforce structure in your objects.

They can be implemented by classes and extended from
other interfaces.

They promote code reusability and maintainability. ## 2.
Type Aliases
```

What are Type Aliases?

Type aliases in TypeScript allow you to create a new name for a type. They can represent primitives, unions, tuples, or any other valid TypeScript type. Unlike interfaces, type aliases can also express more complex types with greater flexibility.

Creating Type Aliases

You can create a type alias by using the `type` keyword. Here's a simple example:

```typescript
type Point = { x: number; y: number };
```

Now, `Point` can be used wherever you need to reference this structure:

```typescript
const drawPoint = (point: Point): void => {
console.log(`Drawing point at (${point.x}, ${point.y})`);
};
```

Type Aliases with Unions

One of the most powerful features of type aliases is their ability to create union types. A union type allows a variable to be one of several types. Here's how you can use type aliases to create union types:

```typescript
type Response = "success" | "error" | "loading";
```

```
const fetchData = (): Response => {

return "success"; // This can also be "error" or "loading"

};
```
` ` `

Summary of Type Aliases

Type aliases provide a way to define new names for types in your application.

They can simplify complex type expressions and improve code readability.

They are particularly useful for creating union types. ## 3. Union Types

What are Union Types?

Union types allow you to define a variable that can hold multiple types. This is especially useful in situations where a function might return different outcomes or when an input can be of various types.

Using Union Types

Here's how to declare a variable that can accept multiple types:

```typescript
function logId(id: number | string): void {
console.log(`ID: ${id}`);

}
```
` ` `

In this example, the `logId` function can accept either a `number` or a `string`. TypeScript will perform type checking to ensure that the right types are being passed.

Advanced Use Cases

Union types can also be used in conjunction with interfaces and type aliases for more complex data handling. For example:

```typescript
interface Dog {
bark: () => void;
}
interface Cat { meow: () => void;
}
type Pet = Dog | Cat;
function playWithPet(pet: Pet): void { if ('bark' in pet) {
pet.bark();
} else {
pet.meow();


}
}
```

In this scenario, the `playWithPet` function can accept either a `Dog` or a `Cat`, and TypeScript allows you to use type guards to check which type is passed.

Summary of Union Types

Union types enable a variable to have multiple potential types.

They enhance flexibility in function parameters and return types.

They can be combined with interfaces and type aliases for more complex structures.

By leveraging these tools, web developers can harness the full potential of TypeScript, ensuring their code is robust and resilient while being easier to read and debug.

Chapter 3: Advanced TypeScript Features

In this chapter, we will explore several advanced TypeScript features, including generics, mapped types, conditional types, type inference, decorators, and more. By the end, you'll have a solid understanding of how to leverage these features to write more robust applications.

3.1 Generics

Generics are one of the most powerful features in TypeScript, allowing developers to create reusable and flexible components. They enable us to write functions, classes, and interfaces that can operate on a variety of types without losing the benefits of type safety.

3.1.1 Generic Functions

Here's an example of a simple generic function that takes an array of elements and returns a single element. The generic type `T` represents the type of elements in the array:

```typescript
function identity<T>(arg: T): T { return arg;

}

let output1 = identity<string>("Hello, TypeScript!"); let output2 = identity<number>(42);
```

In this example, the `identity` function can accept any type, and TypeScript will maintain type safety throughout.

3.1.2 Generic Interfaces and Classes

42

You can use generics in interfaces and classes as well. This allows for the definition of types that work with multiple data types:

```typescript
interface Pair<K, V> { key: K;

value: V;

}

class KeyValuePair<K, V> implements Pair<K, V> {
constructor(public key: K, public value: V) {}

}

const pair = new KeyValuePair<number, string>(1, "One");
```

3.1.3 Constraints

Sometimes, you may want to limit the types that can be used as a generic. This is where constraints come into play. You can enforce that a type extends another type:

```typescript
function loggingIdentity<T extends { length: number }>(arg: T): T { console.log(arg.length);

return arg;

}

loggingIdentity([1, 2, 3]);
```

3.2 Mapped Types

Mapped types enable transformations of existing types. This allows for concise declarations and code that is more expressive.

3.2.1 Creating Mapped Types

You can create a mapped type by iterating over the keys of an existing type:

```typescript
type OptionsFlags<Type> = { [Property in keyof Type]: boolean;
};

type FeatureFlags = { darkMode: () => void; newUserProfile: () => void;
};

type FeatureOptions = OptionsFlags<FeatureFlags>;
```

In this example, `FeatureOptions` will be a type where all properties of `FeatureFlags` are transformed into boolean values. This can be used to toggle features on or off easily.

3.3 Conditional Types

Conditional types help create types based on conditions. They allow for powerful type manipulations:

```typescript
type IsString<T> = T extends string ? "Yes" : "No";

type Result1 = IsString<string>; // "Yes" type Result2 = IsString<number>; // "No"
```

```
```

Conditional types enable more dynamic and adaptive types, improving code versatility. ## 3.4 Type Inference

Type inference is another powerful capability that TypeScript provides. It allows the language to automatically deduce the type of a variable based on its value or context, reducing redundancy.

3.4.1 Implicit Type Inference

When you declare a variable using `const` or `let`, TypeScript can infer its type:

```typescript
let numberValue = 10; // TypeScript infers number type
let stringValue = "Hello"; // Infers string type
```

3.4.2 Contextual Typing

Contextual typing enables TypeScript to infer types based on the surrounding context, such as function parameters:

```typescript
window.onmousedown = (event) => {

console.log(event.button); // TypeScript infers 'event' as MouseEvent

};
```

3.5 Decorators

Decorators are a special kind of declaration that can be attached to classes, methods, accessor properties, or parameters. They offer a way to modify the behavior of these constructs.

3.5.1 Class Decorators

Here's a simple example of a class decorator:

```typescript
function logClass(target: any) { console.log(`Class created: ${target.name}`);
}
@logClass class User {
constructor(public name: string) {}
}
```

3.5.2 Method Decorators

You can also create method decorators to log calls or modify the method's behavior:

```typescript
function logMethod(target: any, propertyKey: string, descriptor: PropertyDescriptor) { const originalMethod = descriptor.value;
descriptor.value = function (...args: any[]) {
console.log(`Call: ${propertyKey} with args: ${JSON.stringify(args)}`);                return originalMethod.apply(this, args);
};
}
```

```
class Calculator { @logMethod
add(x: number, y: number): number { return x + y;
}


}
```
` ` `

By leveraging generics, mapped types, conditional types, type inference, and decorators, developers can create more reusable, maintainable, and type-safe code. These topics lay the groundwork for developing sophisticated applications while maximizing the benefits of TypeScript's static typing system. In the next chapter, we will delve into integrating TypeScript with popular frameworks and libraries, enhancing our understanding of practical TypeScript application.

Mastering Generics for Reusable and Scalable Code

TypeScript, a superset of JavaScript, offers powerful features that enhance productivity and code quality, one of which is generics. In this chapter, we will explore the concept of generics in TypeScript, emphasizing their importance in creating reusable and scalable web applications.

Understanding Generics

Generics enable you to define functions, classes, and interfaces with type parameters. This allows you to create components that can work with any data type while retaining type safety. Generics provide a way to avoid code duplication and enhance the flexibility of components.

Why Use Generics?

Code Reusability: Instead of writing multiple versions of a function for different data types, you can create a single, generic function that adapts to various inputs.

Type Safety: Generics provide compile-time type checking, allowing developers to catch errors early in the development process.

Scalability: As your application grows, using generics can help manage complexity by promoting uniformity across components.

Syntax of Generics in TypeScript

The basic syntax for defining a generic function is as follows:

```typescript
function identity<T>(arg: T): T { return arg;

}
```

In this example:

`T` is a type parameter that represents any type.

The function `identity` takes an argument of type `T` and returns the same type. You can call the `identity` function with different types:

```typescript
let numberOutput = identity<number>(42); //
```

numberOutput: number

let stringOutput = identity<string>("Hello, Generics!"); // stringOutput: string
```

### Generic Interfaces

You can also use generics in interfaces, allowing for more dynamic data structures:

```typescript
interface Pair<K, V> { key: K;

value: V;

}
const pair: Pair<number, string> = { key: 1,

value: "One"

};
```

In this example, the `Pair` interface is defined with two type parameters `K` and `V`, representing the types of the key and value, respectively.

Advanced Generics ### Generic Classes

Classes can also leverage generics, enabling the creation of data structures that can operate on various types:

```typescript class Box<T> {

private contents: T;

constructor(value: T) { this.contents = value;

```
}
getContents(): T { return this.contents;
}
}
const box = new Box<string>("My Box Content");
console.log(box.getContents()); // Output: My Box
Content
```

Constraints in Generics

Sometimes, it makes sense to restrict the types that can be passed to a generic function or class. TypeScript allows for this through constraints:

```typescript
function logLength<T extends { length: number }>(arg:
T): void { console.log(arg.length);
}
logLength("Hello"); // Valid logLength([1, 2, 3]); // Valid
// logLength(123); // Invalid, as numbers don't have a
'length'
```

In this instance, `T` must have a `length` property, ensuring that any arguments passed to `logLength` conform to this structure.

Using Generics with Async Programming

Generics are also useful in working with promises,

particularly in TypeScript's asynchronous programming model:

```typescript
function fetchData<T>(url: string): Promise<T> { return
fetch(url).then(response => response.json());
}
interface User { id: number; name: string;
}
fetchData<User>('https://api.example.com/users/1')
.then(data => { console.log(data.id, data.name);
});
```

In the example above, `fetchData` can fetch data of any type, leveraging generics while ensuring type safety. ## Practical Applications of Generics in Web Development

Building Reusable Components

In modern web development frameworks like Angular, React, or Vue.js, generics allow developers to create reusable components that can accept different data types.

For instance, consider a simple generic component in React:

```tsx
import React from 'react';
interface ListProps<T> { items: T[];
}
```

```typescript
function List<T>({ items }: ListProps<T>): JSX.Element {
return (
<ul>
{items.map((item, index) => (
<li key={index}>{item}</li>
))}
</ul>
);
}
// Usage
<List items={[1, 2, 3]} ></List>

<List items={['Apple', 'Banana']} ></List>
```

Improving API Interactions

When calling APIs, generics can ensure that your data handling functions are robust. For instance, using a generic type for handling API responses can prevent errors from incorrect assumptions about the returned data structure.

```typescript
type ApiResponse<T> = { status: 'success' | 'error'; data: T;
};
const         processResponse      =          <T>(response:
```

```
ApiResponse<T>) => { if (response.status === 'success') {
console.log('Data:', response.data);
} else {
console.error('Error fetching data');
}
};
```
```

By understanding generics' foundational concepts, syntax, and advanced applications, programmers can build robust, type-safe applications that can adapt to changing requirements without sacrificing maintainability.

# Exploring Modules and Namespaces for Code Organization

This chapter delves into two key features of TypeScript: modules and namespaces. We will explore how these features can enhance code organization, promote reusability, and improve maintainability in web development projects.

## Understanding Modules ### What are Modules?

Modules are a way to encapsulate code in TypeScript and JavaScript, promoting better organization and reusability. A module is essentially a file that contains related code. This code can include functions, classes, and interfaces that can be exported and imported in other modules, creating a clear separation of concerns.

### Benefits of Using Modules
```

Encapsulation: By grouping related functionalities into modules, you can hide implementation details and expose only what is necessary.

Reusability: Modules can be imported and reused across different parts of an application, reducing code duplication.

Maintainability: A modular structure makes it easier to manage and update parts of the codebase.

Dependency Management: Well-designed modules make it easier to track and manage dependencies among various parts of the application.

Creating and Using Modules

In TypeScript, you create a module by defining a file that exports components. Here's a simple example:

File: math.ts

```typescript
export function add(a: number, b: number): number {
return a + b;
}

export function subtract(a: number, b: number): number {
return a - b;
}
```

File: app.ts

```typescript
```

```
import { add, subtract } from './math';
console.log(add(5, 3)); // Output: 8
console.log(subtract(5, 3)); // Output: 2
```

In this example, the `math.ts` file defines two functions and exports them. The `app.ts` file then imports these functions, demonstrating how modules facilitate code organization.

Understanding Namespaces ### What are Namespaces?

Namespaces provide a way to group related code together, similar to modules. They were more common in earlier versions of TypeScript but are still useful for organizing code, especially in larger applications. A namespace allows you to create a logical grouping of code without worrying about file or module structure.

Benefits of Using Namespaces

Logical Grouping: Namespaces help in logically grouping related functions and variables under a common identifier, reducing naming collisions.

Clarity: By using namespaces, you can clarify the purpose of the code and its organization.

Simplicity: In smaller projects, namespaces can simplify code structure, allowing developers to avoid creating many small files.

Creating and Using Namespaces

Namespaces are defined using the `namespace` keyword. Here's an example:

File: geometry.ts

```typescript
namespace Geometry {

export function areaOfCircle(radius: number): number {
return Math.PI * radius * radius;

}

export function perimeterOfCircle(radius: number): number { return 2 * Math.PI * radius;

}

}
```

File: app.ts

```typescript
console.log(Geometry.areaOfCircle(5));    // Output: 78.53981633974483
console.log(Geometry.perimeterOfCircle(5)); // Output: 31.41592653589793
```

In this example, the `geometry.ts` file defines a namespace called `Geometry`, encapsulating related functions that calculate areas and perimeters of circles. The `app.ts` file accesses these functions using the namespace, demonstrating how namespaces can help organize related functionalities.

Modules vs. Namespaces: When to Use Each

While both modules and namespaces serve to organize code, they have different use-cases:

Modules: Use modules when you are building larger applications that benefit from dependencies being managed through the ES6 module system. Modules are external and can be better suited for interactions with bundlers like Webpack, which is common in modern web development.

Namespaces: Consider namespaces for smaller codebases or when working on legacy systems that may not support modules fully. They are also useful for grouping logically related functionalities without the need for multiple files.

Best Practices for Code Organization

Keep Modules Focused: Each module should ideally encapsulate a single responsibility, making it easier to maintain.

Use Descriptive Names: When naming modules and namespaces, use clear and descriptive names to make the codebase more understandable.

Limit Namespace Usage: Favor modules over namespaces in larger applications to align with modern JavaScript practices.

Document Modules and Namespaces: Including comments and documentation can aid in understanding the purpose and usage of different modules and namespaces.

By leveraging modules for encapsulation and reusability and using namespaces for logical grouping of related functionalities, developers can create maintainable and scalable applications. Understanding when to use modules versus namespaces and adhering to best practices can lead to a more organized and efficient codebase, ultimately resulting in a better development experience.

Chapter 4: TypeScript and JavaScript Interoperability

However, as applications have grown increasingly complex, developers have sought alternatives and enhancements to improve maintainability, type safety, and tooling. TypeScript, a superset of JavaScript developed by Microsoft, has emerged as a powerful tool, allowing developers to harness the flexibility of JavaScript while adding static types.

This chapter delves into the interplay between TypeScript and JavaScript, exploring how these two languages can coexist, enhance each other, and provide a robust development experience.

4.1 Understanding TypeScript

Before diving into interoperability, it's essential to grasp the fundamentals of TypeScript. TypeScript offers a rich type system, interfaces, enums, and access modifiers, allowing developers to define data structures and function contracts more explicitly. This clarity in code definition enables better tooling, such as autocompletion and refactoring support in IDEs, and assists in catching type-related errors at compile time, rather than runtime.

4.1.1 Type Inference and Annotations

One of TypeScript's notable features is its type inference. It can automatically infer types based on the values assigned to variables, reducing the need for extensive type annotations. However, developers can still leverage explicit type annotations for clarity:

```typescript
```

```
let num: number = 42; // Explicit annotation

let inferredNum = 42; // TypeScript infers 'number'
```

This capability allows teams to introduce TypeScript incrementally into existing JavaScript projects without the need for a complete rewrite.

4.2 Interoperability Fundamentals

Interoperability between TypeScript and JavaScript is a critical aspect of utilizing TypeScript in existing codebases. Since TypeScript is designed to be a superset of JavaScript, any valid JavaScript code is also valid TypeScript code. This seamless integration allows developers to progressively enhance their JavaScript projects by adding TypeScript files.

4.2.1 Using TypeScript in a JavaScript Project

To integrate TypeScript into a JavaScript project, the first step is to install TypeScript using npm:

```bash
npm install --save-dev typescript
```

Next, developers can create a `tsconfig.json` file to configure TypeScript's behavior. A simple configuration may look like this:

```json
{
"compilerOptions": { "target": "es5", "module": "commonjs", "strict": true
```

```
}
}
```
```

This setup enables strict type checking, targets ES5 for broader browser compatibility, and uses CommonJS modules.

### 4.2.2 Mixing TypeScript and JavaScript Files

Once TypeScript is set up, developers can begin writing `.ts` files alongside their traditional `.js` files. TypeScript can easily understand and type-check JavaScript code. For example, in a JavaScript file:

```javascript
// greeting.js
function greet(name) { return `Hello, ${name}!`;
}
module.exports = greet;
```

In a TypeScript file, you can import and use this function with type safety:

```typescript
// main.ts
import greet from './greeting';
const name: string = 'World'; console.log(grcct(name));
```

This way, TypeScript provides type checking for the
```

JavaScript function, enforcing the expected types at compile time.

4.3 Type Definitions

To fully utilize JavaScript libraries in TypeScript, type definitions are crucial. These definitions provide TypeScript with the information it needs to type-check JavaScript libraries correctly. Depending on the library's complexity and community support, type definitions may come from several sources:

4.3.1 DefinitelyTyped

The DefinitelyTyped repository hosts thousands of type definitions for JavaScript libraries. Developers can install types using npm:

```bash
npm install --save-dev @types/[library-name]
```

For example, to add type definitions for jQuery:

```bash
npm install --save-dev @types/jquery
```

4.3.2 Inline Type Declarations

For smaller or custom libraries without existing type declarations, developers can provide inline type declarations:

```typescript
declare module 'my-library' {
```

```
export function myFunction(param: string): number;
}
```
```

These declarations allow TypeScript to understand the shapes of objects and functions from non-TypeScript libraries.

## 4.4 Transitioning to TypeScript

For teams looking to transition from JavaScript to TypeScript, a gradual approach is often the most effective. Start by converting individual files or modules, writing TypeScript files where possible, and allowing JavaScript to remain for the time being. Eventually, as more parts of the codebase are converted, type safety will improve, leading to fewer runtime errors and a more maintainable codebase.

Key steps to facilitate this transition include:

**Identify critical components**: Begin with the most important or most commonly used parts of the application.

**Incremental type checking**: Use the `allowJs` option in `tsconfig.json` to enable type checking for both `.js` and `.ts` files.

**Adopt strict mode**: Enable strict mode in TypeScript for maximum type safety. ## 4.5 Challenges of Interoperability

While TypeScript and JavaScript interoperability is immensely beneficial, it does come with its challenges:

**Complex libraries**: Some JavaScript libraries may

63
```

have extensive API surfaces that are challenging to represent accurately with TypeScript types.

Dynamic nature of JavaScript: JavaScript's dynamic typing can lead to situations where legitimate type errors slip through when integrating with TypeScript.

To mitigate these challenges, developers should embrace thorough testing and consider using tools like linters and type checkers to catch issues before they surface.

As TypeScript continues to gain traction in the developer community, its ability to coexist with JavaScript will enable teams to incrementally adopt its features, leading to cleaner, more maintainable codebases.

Understanding how to leverage this interoperability will be an invaluable asset in any modern development toolkit, paving the way for future innovations in the JavaScript ecosystem..

Using TypeScript with JavaScript: Gradual Adoption Strategies

This chapter aims to provide practical strategies for gradual adoption of TypeScript in JavaScript projects, ensuring a smooth transition without overwhelming developers or disrupting existing workflows.

Understanding TypeScript's Advantages

Before diving into adoption strategies, it's essential to

recognize why TypeScript is gaining popularity. Some core benefits include:

Static Typing: Developers can catch errors during development rather than at runtime, leading to more reliable code.

Improved IDE Support: TypeScript's static types enhance auto-completion, navigation, and refactoring capabilities in modern IDEs, making coding more efficient.

Modern Features: TypeScript incorporates features from ESNext such as async/await, interfaces, enums, and more, which can make code cleaner and more organized.

Seamless Interoperability: TypeScript can work alongside JavaScript, allowing developers to adopt it incrementally without needing to rewrite entire codebases.

Understanding these benefits can help in advocating for TypeScript within your team or organization, setting the stage for a smooth introduction.

Strategy 1: Start with TypeScript Gradually ### 1.1. Configuration and Basic Setup

The first step towards integrating TypeScript is to set up a TypeScript compiler. Starting with a partial configuration allows for easy initial adoption:

- **Install TypeScript**: Use npm or yarn to add TypeScript to your project.

```bash
npm install --save-dev typescript
```

```
```

- **Create a `tsconfig.json` file**: This file contains compiler options. Start with a basic configuration:

```json
{
"compilerOptions": { "target": "es5", "module": "commonjs", "strict": true, "esModuleInterop": true
},
"include": ["src/**/*"], "exclude": ["node_modules"]
}
```

1.2. Converting Files to TypeScript

Instead of converting the entire codebase at once, consider changing file extensions from `.js` to `.ts` one at a time. Start with simple utility functions or modules that are less complex. This allows developers to test TypeScript features gradually without the pressure of refactoring large portions of the codebase.

1.3. Use `// @ts-check`

For projects where TypeScript is not fully adopted, you can introduce type checking in JavaScript files by adding `// @ts-check` at the top of your JavaScript files. This enables TypeScript to provide type checking and intelligent suggestions without converting the file to TypeScript, offering an easy way to experience TypeScript's benefits in a gradual manner.

Strategy 2: Leveraging Type Definitions

Type definitions are critical when integrating TypeScript into an existing JavaScript codebase. Using DefinitelyTyped, a repository of type definitions for JavaScript libraries, developers can easily add type safety to third-party libraries, enabling better type-checking without converting every file.

2.1. Installing Type Definitions

To install type definitions for a library, you can use npm:

```bash
npm install --save-dev @types/library-name
```

This allows the TypeScript compiler to understand how to process the external library's API, enhancing your JavaScript code with type safety. It's beneficial to start using well-defined libraries where typings exist, as it reduces the complexity of transitioning.

2.2. Creating Custom Type Definitions

In cases where type definitions do not exist, developers can create custom declaration files (`*.d.ts`) which provide the compiler with information about the shapes and types of the JavaScript objects. This step allows teams to maintain type safety without needing to rewrite existing functionality immediately.

Strategy 3: Phased Migration ### 3.1. Project Structure

Keeping your project organized is critical during migration. Consider splitting your project into manageable chunks, where you can shift sections to TypeScript as resources allow. For example, structural divisions (modules, components) or features can be prioritized based on their importance or complexity.

3.2. Prioritize Core Functionality

When migrating, focus on core functionality first. Components that are frequently modified or critical to the application's operation should be prioritized for conversion. This approach enhances overall stability and provides more immediate benefits from type safety.

Strategy 4: Training and Documentation

One of the challenges of adopting TypeScript is ensuring that developers are comfortable with its paradigms. Providing training resources and documentation can significantly ease the transition:

Workshops and Pair Programming: Conduct sessions aimed at demonstrating TypeScript's benefits, showcasing best practices, and practical code reviews in TypeScript.

Internal Documentation: Create a style guide or best practices document tailored to your team's standards and practices when using TypeScript.

With a mindful approach, developers can gradually shift their codebases towards TypeScript, driving greater efficiency, maintainability, and productivity in their future projects. Whether you're working on a legacy application or starting a new project, these gradual adoption strategies can pave the way for a successful integration of TypeScript into your development workflow.

Working with Third-Party JavaScript Libraries in TypeScript

This chapter aims to provide a comprehensive guide for seamlessly integrating third-party JavaScript libraries into TypeScript projects.

Understanding Type Definitions

In TypeScript, working with third-party libraries requires an understanding of type definitions. Libraries written in plain JavaScript do not include type information. To bridge this gap, TypeScript uses type definition files, which are typically recognized by the `.d.ts` suffix. These files describe the types and structures of the code in the library, allowing TypeScript to perform type checking and provide better IntelliSense support in editors.

Installing Type Definitions

Many popular JavaScript libraries have type definitions available through DefinitelyTyped, a community-contributed repository for type definitions. The types can be installed using npm (Node Package Manager) with the following command:

```bash
npm install --save-dev @types/library-name
```

For example, to install type definitions for jQuery, you would run:

```bash
npm install --save-dev @types/jquery
```

```
```

When using libraries that do not have existing type definitions, you have the option to create your own definitions or utilize the `any` type to bypass type checking temporarily.

Importing Third-Party Libraries

After installing a library and its type definitions, you can import it into your TypeScript files. For CommonJS modules (such as Node.js packages), you typically use the `require` function. For ES6 style imports, you can use the `import` statement.

Example with ES6 Import

For instance, if you are using a library like Lodash, which has type definitions:

```typescript
import * as _ from 'lodash';

const numbers: number[] = [1, 2, 3, 4, 5]; const
shuffledNumbers          =          _.shuffle(numbers);
console.log(shuffledNumbers);
```

Example with CommonJS Require

If the library does not have type definitions, you might resort to using `require`:

```typescript
const moment = require('moment');

const now = moment().format('MMMM Do YYYY,
h:mm:ss a'); console.log(now);
```

```
```

Creating Custom Type Definitions

If you encounter a library that does not provide type definitions, you can create your own. This is done by defining a `.d.ts` file where you describe the types and interfaces for the library's API.

Example: Creating a Custom Type Definition

For example, if you are using a custom library called `myLibrary` with a function called `doStuff`, you can create a `myLibrary.d.ts` file:

```typescript
declare module 'myLibrary' {

export function doStuff(param: string): number;

}
```

Once you've defined the types, you can use `myLibrary` in your TypeScript code like this:

```typescript
import { doStuff } from 'myLibrary';

const result = doStuff("test"); console.log(result); // type-safe
```

Using the `any` Type and @ts-ignore

While TypeScript's strict typing is beneficial, sometimes you may need to interact with a library without type definitions. In such cases, you can use `any` as a

71

placeholder type.

Example of Using `any`

```typescript
declare const myGlobalLib: any;
const result = myGlobalLib.someFunction();
```

Alternatively, you can ignore TypeScript errors for a specific line by using `// @ts-ignore`. This should be used sparingly since it bypasses type checking:

```typescript
// @ts-ignore
const result = myUnknownLibrary.someMethod();
```

Type Assertion

When working with libraries lacking type definitions, you can also leverage type assertions to inform TypeScript of the variable's type. This provides a way to express your intentions safely.

Example of Type Assertion

```typescript
const result = myGlobalLib as { someFunction: () => number }; const numberResult = result.someFunction();
```

By utilizing type definitions, creating custom typings, and

strategically employing the `any` type, developers can effectively combine the strengths of TypeScript with the vast ecosystem of JavaScript libraries. As you gain experience in using TypeScript alongside these libraries, you'll appreciate the enhanced safety, autocompletion, and documentation that TypeScript provides, empowering you to write robust, maintainable code.

Chapter 5: TypeScript for the DOM and Web APIs

In this chapter, we will explore how TypeScript enhances the experience of working with the Document Object Model (DOM) and various Web APIs, helping developers to create more robust, maintainable, and type-safe code.

5.1 Understanding the DOM and Web APIs

The Document Object Model (DOM) is a programming interface provided by web browsers that allows scripts to dynamically access and manipulate the content and structure of a web document. It represents the document as a tree of objects, where each node corresponds to a part of the document, such as elements, attributes, and text nodes.

Web APIs, on the other hand, are a collection of methods and interfaces that allow developers to perform complex operations in a web environment without dealing directly with the underlying implementation. These APIs enable functionalities like fetching data from a server, manipulating multimedia content, and interacting with the browser itself.

5.2 Setting Up TypeScript for DOM Manipulation

Before diving into TypeScript, we need to set up our development environment. If you haven't already, install TypeScript globally using npm:

```bash
npm install -g typescript
```

Next, create a new project directory and initialize a `tsconfig.json` file:

```bash
mkdir my-typescript-project cd my-typescript-project

tsc --init
```

Now, you can create a file named `index.ts` where you will write your TypeScript code. The TypeScript compiler will handle type checking and transpile your TypeScript code into JavaScript, ensuring compatibility with all modern browsers.

5.3 Type Safety with the DOM

One of the key benefits of using TypeScript is its type safety. When interacting with the DOM, TypeScript allows you to define specific types for elements, reducing the likelihood of runtime errors caused by null or undefined values. Consider the following example:

```typescript
const button = document.getElementById('submitButton') as HTMLButtonElement;

button.addEventListener('click', () => {
  console.log('Button clicked!');
});
```

In this code snippet, we use a type assertion to indicate that we expect the `getElementById` method to return an

`HTMLButtonElement`. This ensures that TypeScript will alert us if we attempt to use properties or methods that do not exist on the `HTMLButtonElement` interface.

5.4 Working with Different HTML Elements

TypeScript supports a wide variety of HTML elements, each with its own unique properties and methods. By leveraging these types, you can write more descriptive and error-resistant code. Here's how you might handle a text input field:

```typescript
const input = document.getElementById('textInput') as HTMLInputElement;

input.addEventListener('input', () => {
console.log(`Current value: ${input.value}`);
});
```

In this case, asserting that `input` is an `HTMLInputElement` provides access to specific properties like

`value`, ensuring a safer interaction with the DOM. ## 5.5 Utilizing Web APIs

TypeScript also simplifies working with Web APIs by offering strong typings for methods and responses. One common use case is fetching data using the Fetch API, which returns a Promise. Here's an example:

```typescript
async function fetchData(url: string): Promise<void> { try {
```

```
const response = await fetch(url); if (!response.ok) {
throw new Error('Network response was not ok');
}
const data = await response.json(); console.log(data);
} catch (error) {
console.error('There was a problem with the fetch operation:', error);
}
}
fetchData('https://api.example.com/data');
```

In this example, using the Fetch API is made more robust with error handling, and TypeScript's type inference helps us manage the response shape with more ease.

5.6 Creating Custom Types and Interfaces

To further enhance type safety, you can define custom types and interfaces for complex objects returned from Web APIs. For instance, if you're fetching user data, you might create an interface:

```typescript
interface User {
id: number; name: string; email: string;
}
async function fetchUserData(url: string): Promise<User[]> { const response = await fetch(url);
return await response.json() as User[];
```

```
}
fetchUserData('https://api.example.com/users')
.then(users => { users.forEach(user => {
console.log(`User: ${user.name} (${user.email})`);
});
});
```

By defining the `User` interface, you ensure that the expected shape of the data is consistent throughout your application.

TypeScript provides developers with powerful tools to work with the DOM and Web APIs, enhancing both the developer experience and application reliability. By adding types, handling errors more gracefully, and defining interfaces for complex objects, you can write cleaner, safer, and more maintainable code.

Strongly-Typed DOM Manipulation and Event Handling

TypeScript, a superset of JavaScript, offers a powerful solution to these challenges through strong typing. This chapter explores the integration of strongly-typed DOM manipulation and event handling in TypeScript, aiming to improve code quality and developer productivity.

1. The Basics of TypeScript

Before diving into DOM manipulation and event handling,

it's essential to understand the foundational concepts of TypeScript.

1.1 What is TypeScript?

TypeScript is a statically typed programming language developed by Microsoft. It adds optional types to JavaScript, enabling developers to catch errors early in the development process and improve code clarity. Key features of TypeScript include:

Static Typing: Helps identify type-related errors during compilation rather than at runtime.

Interfaces and Type Aliases: Allows creating contracts for object shapes, enhancing code reuse and readability.

Enums and Tuples: Offers more advanced data structures than traditional JavaScript. ### 1.2 Setting Up TypeScript

To get started with TypeScript, ensure you have Node.js and npm installed on your machine. You can install TypeScript globally using the following command:

```bash
npm install -g typescript
```

You can then create a new TypeScript file and compile it using the `tsc` command. ## 2. Accessing the DOM with Strong Typing

In JavaScript, accessing the DOM often leads to issues where the element types are not clearly defined. TypeScript allows you to define these elements with specific types, reducing runtime errors.

2.1 Selecting Elements

You can use `document.querySelector` or `document.getElementById` to select DOM elements. In TypeScript, these can be defined with type assertions to ensure strong typing.

```typescript
const button = document.querySelector<HTMLButtonElement>('#myButton'); const input = document.getElementById('myInput') as HTMLInputElement;

if (button && input) { button.textContent = 'Click me!';

input.value = 'Hello, World';

}
```

2.2 Manipulating Element Properties

With TypeScript, manipulating DOM elements becomes safer and more predictable. For instance, if you want to change the text of an element or add an event listener, you can do this with guaranteed types.

```typescript
if (button) {

button.onclick = () => { alert(input.value);

};

}
```

In this example, TypeScript ensures that the `button`

variable is indeed an `HTMLButtonElement`, so you won't mistakenly call a method that doesn't exist on that type.

3. Strongly-Typed Event Handling

DOM events are a crucial part of web applications, and handling them correctly is paramount. TypeScript makes event handling not only more secure but also more readable.

3.1 Typing Event Handlers

TypeScript provides built-in types for standard events, such as `MouseEvent`, `KeyboardEvent`, and others. This helps to define event handlers explicitly.

```typescript
const handleClick = (event: MouseEvent): void => {

console.log(`Clicked at coordinates: (${event.clientX}, ${event.clientY})`);

};

if (button) {

button.addEventListener('click', handleClick);

}
```

Here, the `event` parameter is explicitly typed as `MouseEvent`, giving you access to properties like `clientX` and `clientY`. ### 3.2 Custom Events

Creating custom events is also simplified in TypeScript. You can define a custom event, dispatch it, and handle it with type safety in mind.

```typescript
interface CustomEventDetail { message: string;
}

const customEvent = new CustomEvent<CustomEventDetail>('myCustomEvent', {
detail: { message: 'This is a custom event!' },
});
document.addEventListener('myCustomEvent', (event) => { console.log(event.detail.message);
});
// Dispatch the event
document.dispatchEvent(customEvent);
```

In this case, the detail of the custom event is strongly typed, ensuring that the consumer of the event knows exactly what to expect.

Strongly-typed DOM manipulation and event handling in TypeScript significantly enhance the quality of web applications. By leveraging TypeScript's static typing, developers can write cleaner, safer, and more maintainable code. The clarity gained from these practices leads to fewer bugs and a more enjoyable development experience.

Using Fetch API and Working with JSON in TypeScript

The Fetch API provides a flexible interface for making HTTP requests, and when combined with JSON (JavaScript Object Notation), it allows developers to work with data in a format that is easy to read and manipulate. Using TypeScript enhances the development experience by adding static types, which can help prevent errors and improve code quality. This chapter will explore how to use the Fetch API in a TypeScript environment and how to manage JSON data effectively.

Understanding the Fetch API

The Fetch API is a modern interface for making network requests to servers. It replaces the older

`XMLHttpRequest` and is promise-based, making it easier to work with asynchronous requests. Here's a basic example of how to use Fetch:

```typescript
fetch('https://api.example.com/data')

.then(response => { if (!response.ok) {

throw new Error('Network response was not ok');

}

return response.json(); // Parsing the response as JSON

})

.then(data => console.log(data))

.catch(error => console.error('There was a problem with the fetch operation:', error));
```

```
```

Fetch API Features

Promises: The Fetch API returns a Promise, allowing for cleaner handling of asynchronous code with

`.then()` and `.catch()`.

Readable Response: Fetch returns a Response object, from which you can read the body using methods like `response.json()`, `response.text()`, or `response.blob()`.

Better Handling of CORS: Automatically deals with Cross-Origin Resource Sharing (CORS) issues when configured properly.

Request Configuration: Offers customization options through an options object, allowing developers to specify HTTP methods, headers, body content, and more.

Using Fetch in TypeScript

When leveraging TypeScript, a fundamental aspect is defining the types of data you expect to work with. This helps catch errors at compile time rather than runtime. Let's say you're fetching user data from an API. First, define a type or interface for the data structure:

```typescript
interface User { id: number; name: string; email: string;
}

async function fetchUserData(): Promise<User[]> {

const response = await fetch('https://api.example.com/users');
```

```typescript
if (!response.ok) {

throw new Error('Network response was not ok');

}

const data: User[] = await response.json(); // Type assertion return data;

}

fetchUserData()

.then(users => console.log(users))

.catch(error => console.error('There was a problem fetching user data:', error));
```

Error Handling

Effective error handling is essential for a robust web application. When using the Fetch API, consider both network errors and response errors. You can manage different types of errors gracefully:

```typescript
async function fetchUserDataWithErrorHandling(): Promise<User[]> { try {

const response = await fetch('https://api.example.com/users');


if (!response.ok) {

throw new Error(`HTTP error! Status: ${response.status}`);
```

```
}
const data: User[] = await response.json(); return data;
} catch (error) {
console.error('Error fetching user data:', error); return [];
// Return an empty array on error
}
}
```

Working with JSON in TypeScript

JSON is a common data interchange format, especially in web APIs. TypeScript's type system allows developers to easily work with JSON by defining types that mirror the expected structure of the JSON data.

Parsing JSON

When receiving a response from a Fetch request, it is often in JSON format. The `response.json()` method parses the JSON and converts it into a JavaScript object. Here's an example of how to parse nested JSON:

```typescript
interface Post { id: number;

title: string; body: string;
}
async function fetchPosts(): Promise<Post[]> {
const       response       =       await
fetch('https://api.example.com/posts');
```

```typescript
if (!response.ok) {

throw new Error('Network response was not ok');

}

const posts: Post[] = await response.json(); return posts;

}
```

Sending JSON Data

In addition to fetching data, web applications frequently need to send JSON data to APIs, for instance, when creating or updating records. This requires specifying the right headers and converting your data to a JSON string:

```typescript
async function createPost(newPost: Post): Promise<void>
{         const         response         =         await
fetch('https://api.example.com/posts', { method: 'POST',

headers: {

'Content-Type': 'application/json'

},

body: JSON.stringify(newPost)

});

if (!response.ok) {

throw new Error('Failed to create a new post');

}

console.log('Post created successfully!');

}
```

```
```

By leveraging the fetch functionality, TypeScript's type safety, and JSON's structure, developers can build dynamic web applications that are robust and maintainable. Understanding how to handle requests, parse responses, and ensure type safety is essential to creating excellent user experiences in the ever-evolving landscape of the web.

Chapter 6: Asynchronous Programming with TypeScript

In this chapter, we'll explore the various aspects of asynchronous programming in TypeScript, including Promises, async/await syntax, error handling, and the integration of asynchronous code into our applications.

6.1 Understanding Asynchronous Programming

JavaScript, the language on which TypeScript builds, is inherently single-threaded. This means it has one main execution thread, which makes it efficient for handling tasks like user interactions. However, when it comes to operations that take time to complete, such as API requests, JavaScript's synchronous nature can lead to a poor user experience if not handled properly.

6.1.1 The Event Loop

At the core of JavaScript's asynchronous capabilities lies the event loop. The event loop constantly monitors the call stack and the task queue, allowing the execution of code that is ready to run while waiting for other operations, such as I/O tasks, to complete. This mechanism allows JavaScript to perform non-blocking operations seamlessly.

6.2 Promises

Promises are a foundational aspect of asynchronous programming in TypeScript. A Promise represents the eventual completion (or failure) of an asynchronous operation and its resulting value.

6.2.1 Creating a Promise

Here's how to create a basic Promise in TypeScript:

```typescript
const fetchData = (): Promise<string> => { return new
Promise((resolve, reject) => {

setTimeout(() => {

const data = "Data fetched successfully!"; resolve(data);

}, 2000);

});

};
```

In the example above, `fetchData` returns a Promise that resolves after two seconds. Utilizing Promises effectively allows developers to manage asynchrony more clearly.

6.2.2 Using Promises

To handle the resolved value or error of a Promise, we use `.then()` and `.catch()`. Here's how:

```typescript
fetchData()

.then(data => {


console.log(data); // Output: Data fetched successfully!

})

.catch(error => { console.error("Error:", error);

});
```

This structure enables a cleaner way to deal with asynchronous results, as opposed to deeply nested callbacks.

6.3 Async/Await

Introduced in ES2017, async/await is syntactical sugar over Promises that makes writing asynchronous code easier to understand and maintain.

6.3.1 The `async` Function

To define a function as asynchronous, simply prepend it with the `async` keyword:

```typescript
const fetchDataAsync = async (): Promise<string> => {
return new Promise((resolve) => {

setTimeout(() => {

resolve("Data fetched using async/await!");

}, 2000);

});

};
```

6.3.2 Using the `await` Keyword

The `await` keyword can be used inside an async function to pause execution until the Promise is resolved or rejected:

```typescript
const fetchAndLogData = async () => { try {

const data = await fetchDataAsync();
```

```typescript
console.log(data); // Output: Data fetched using
async/await!
} catch (error) { console.error("Error:", error);
}
};
fetchAndLogData();
```

In the above code, `await` provides a more synchronous-looking code flow, greatly improving readability when dealing with multiple asynchronous operations.

6.4 Error Handling in Asynchronous Code ### 6.4.1 Handling Errors with Promises

Errors in Promises can be caught using `.catch()`, but when using async/await, we can use a try/catch block for more intuitive error handling.

6.4.2 Example of Error Handling

```typescript
const fetchWithError = async (): Promise<string> => {
throw new Error("Failed to fetch data!");
};
const fetchDataWithErrorHandling = async () => { try {
const data = await fetchWithError(); console.log(data);
} catch (error) {
console.error("Caught an error:", error.message);
}
```

```
};
fetchDataWithErrorHandling();
```
```

In this example, the error thrown from `fetchWithError`
is caught in the try/catch block, allowing for graceful error
handling.

## 6.5 Returning Multiple Promises Concurrently

Using `Promise.all()`, you can run multiple Promises
concurrently. This is especially useful for when you need
to perform multiple independent asynchronous tasks.

```typescript
const fetchMultipleData = async () => {

const promises = [fetchDataAsync(), fetchDataAsync(),
fetchDataAsync()]; try {

const results = await Promise.all(promises);
console.log(results); // Array of results

} catch (error) {

console.error("Error during fetching:", error);

}

};

fetchMultipleData();
```
```

In this case, all three `fetchDataAsync` calls are initiated
simultaneously, and execution awaits the resolution of all
Promises before proceeding.

Asynchronous programming is a vital skill for

contemporary web development, especially when building applications that rely on real-time data and responsive design. TypeScript enhances the power of JavaScript by providing static types, enabling developers to write safer, more maintainable asynchronous code.

Mastering Promises, async/await, and Error Handling

This chapter delves into the intricacies of promises, the async/await syntax, and robust error handling strategies that will empower you to master asynchronous programming.

Understanding Promises

At its core, a Promise is an object that represents the eventual completion (or failure) of an asynchronous operation and its resulting value. A promise can be in one of three states:

Pending: The initial state, neither fulfilled nor rejected.

Fulfilled: The operation completed successfully.

Rejected: The operation failed. ### Creating a Promise

Creating a promise requires a function that takes two parameters: `resolve` and `reject`. Here's a simple example:

```javascript
const myPromise = new Promise((resolve, reject) => {
const success = true; // Simulating success or failure if
```

```
(success) {
resolve("Operation succeeded!");
} else {
reject("Operation failed!");
}
});
```

Consuming a Promise

To consume a promise, you can use the `then()` method to handle fulfillment and the `catch()` method to handle rejection:

```javascript
myPromise
.then((result) => {
console.log(result); // Output: "Operation succeeded!"
})
.catch((error) => { console.error(error);
});
```

Chaining Promises

One of the powerful features of promises is their ability to be chained. Each `then()` returns a new promise, allowing for a sequence of asynchronous operations:

```javascript
fetch('https://jsonplaceholder.typicode.com/todos/1')
```

```
.then(response => response.json())
.then(data => {
console.log(data.title); // Output: Title of the todo item
})
.catch(err => console.error('Error fetching data:', err));
```

The async/await Syntax

In ES2017, JavaScript introduced the `async` and `await` keywords, which provide a more intuitive way to write asynchronous code. Using `async/await` can often make your code easier to read and maintain.

Declaring an Async Function

An `async` function is a function declared with the `async` keyword, which allows you to use `await` inside it. Here's an example:

```javascript
async function fetchData() {

const response = await fetch('https://jsonplaceholder.typicode.com/todos/1');
const data = await response.json();

console.log(data.title);

}
```

Error Handling with Async/Await

Handling errors in an async function can be elegantly managed with `try...catch`. This allows you to catch any

96

errors that occur during the awaited operations.

```javascript
async function fetchData() { try {

const response = await fetch('https://jsonplaceholder.typicode.com/todos/1'); if (!response.ok) {

throw new Error('Network response was not ok');

}

const data = await response.json(); console.log(data.title);

} catch (error) {

console.error('Error fetching data:', error);

}

}
```

Combining Promises, Async/Await, and Error Handling

While both promises and async/await are powerful on their own, understanding how to integrate them is crucial. You can return a promise from an async function, allowing you to mix both styles.

```javascript
const getData = async (url) => {


const response = await fetch(url); if (!response.ok) {

throw new Error('Network response was not ok');
```

```
}
return response.json();
};
getData('https://jsonplaceholder.typicode.com/todos/1')
.then(data => console.log(data.title))
.catch(err => console.error('Error:', err));
```
```

## Best Practices for Error Handling

Effective error handling is vital in asynchronous programming. Here are some best practices: ### 1. Always Handle Errors

Whether you're using promises or async/await, always have a mechanism to catch and respond to errors. ### 2. Use Specific Error Messages

When throwing or logging errors, provide clear and specific messages. This will help with debugging. ### 3. Avoid Silent Failures

Make sure that your code does not fail silently. For example, if a promise is rejected, ensure you have a catch block or a try/catch in place that will alert you to the problem.

### 4. Clean Up Resources

If your async operations involve resources that need to be cleaned up, such as timers or network requests, ensure that you handle cleanup in case of errors.

With a deep understanding of these concepts, you can tackle complex web applications, enhance user experience
```

with smoother interactions, and elevate your capabilities as a developer. As you continue to build your expertise, remember that practice and patience are fundamental in mastering asynchronous programming in JavaScript.

Leveraging TypeScript with RxJS for Reactive Programming

This chapter delves into how TypeScript can be integrated with Reactive Extensions for JavaScript (RxJS) to create robust reactive applications.

Understanding Reactive Programming

At its core, reactive programming is about working with asynchronous streams of data. Unlike traditional imperative programming, where the flow of the program is controlled sequentially, reactive programming allows developers to react to events, such as user inputs or data updates, as they occur. In web applications, this is particularly useful due to the inherently asynchronous nature of things like API calls, user interactions, and real-time data feeds.

Reactive programming treats data as streams that can be observed and manipulated. This brings forth powerful abstractions such as Observables, which can emit data over time and enable developers to subscribe to those changes, executing logic whenever new data is available.

The Role of RxJS

RxJS is a powerful library for reactive programming using Observables. It provides a rich set of operators to create, transform, filter, and combine streams of data elegantly.

Some of its key features include:

Observables: The core building block, representing a stream of data that can be observed.

Operators: Functions that enable complex stream manipulations, including mapping, filtering, and reducing.

Schedulers: Allowing control over the timing and execution of observable operations.

By utilizing RxJS, developers can simplify asynchronous operations, manage event streams, and create clean, maintainable code.

Types and Type Inference in TypeScript

TypeScript enhances JavaScript by providing static typing. This feature is invaluable when building large- scale applications, as it helps catch errors at compile-time rather than runtime. Type inference in TypeScript allows the compiler to deduce types automatically, further reducing the need for explicit type declarations.

In the context of RxJS, TypeScript ensures that developers are explicitly aware of the data types flowing through their streams. This leads to:

Type Safety: Ensuring that the data being processed conforms to expected types, preventing runtime errors.

Enhanced Autocompletion: Better support in IDEs for method suggestions, parameter types, and return types, improving developer productivity.

Clearer Intent: Making the codebase more maintainable by clearly indicating the shape of data being manipulated.

Setting Up TypeScript with RxJS

To get started, we need to set up a basic project incorporating TypeScript and RxJS. Below are the steps to set up the environment:

1. Project Initialization

Start by creating a new project directory and initializing it as a Node.js project:

```bash
mkdir rxjs-typescript-demo cd rxjs-typescript-demo npm init -y
```

2. Installing Dependencies

Next, install TypeScript and RxJS along with some types that will enhance the TypeScript experience:

```bash
npm install typescript rxjs

npm install @types/node --save-dev
```

3. Configuring TypeScript

Create a `tsconfig.json` file to configure TypeScript options:

```json
{
"compilerOptions": { "target": "ES6", "module": "commonjs", "strict": true, "esModuleInterop": true, "skipLibCheck": true
```

```
},
"include": ["src/**/*"], "exclude": ["node_modules"]
}
```

4. Creating an Observable Example

In the `src` directory, create a file named `index.ts` and include the following sample code demonstrating the use of RxJS:

```typescript
import { Observable } from 'rxjs';

// Create an observable that emits a sequence of numbers

const numberObservable: Observable<number> = new Observable<number>((observer) => { let count = 0;

const intervalId = setInterval(() => { if (count < 5) {
observer.next(count++);


} else { observer.complete(); clearInterval(intervalId);
}
}, 1000);
});

//            Subscribe            to            the            observable
numberObservable.subscribe({ next(num) {

console.log(`Received number: ${num}`);
},
complete() {
```

```
console.log('Observable completed');
}
});
```

5. Building and Running the Application Add a build script to the `package.json`:

```json
"scripts": { "build": "tsc",
"start": "node dist/index.js"
}
```

Now run the following commands to build and start the application:

```bash
npm run build npm start
```

You should see sequences of numbers printed to the console every second until it completes. ## Advanced Operators and Patterns

Combining Streams

One of the most powerful aspects of RxJS is its ability to combine multiple streams. Utilizing operators like

`merge`, `combineLatest`, and `forkJoin` allows developers to create complex yet efficient data flows.

```typescript
import { combineLatest, of } from 'rxjs'; import { map }
```

```typescript
from 'rxjs/operators';
// Sample observables const obs1 = of(1, 2, 3);
const obs2 = of('A', 'B', 'C');
// Combine latest observables combineLatest([obs1,
obs2]).pipe( map(([num, char]) => `${num}${char}`)
).subscribe(result => console.log(result));
```

Error Handling

Proper error handling in async flows is essential. Using the `catchError` operator allows you to handle errors gracefully within your streams.

```typescript
import { throwError, of } from 'rxjs'; import { catchError }
from 'rxjs/operators';

const failingObservable = throwError('An error
occurred!'); failingObservable.pipe(

catchError(err => {

console.error(err);

return of('Fallback value'); // Return a fallback observable

})

).subscribe(value => console.log(value));
```

The type safety offered by TypeScript enhances the development process, allowing developers to catch errors early and convey clear intentions through their code. Applying RxJS's powerful set of operators and observable patterns enables the creation of responsive applications that elegantly handle asynchronous data streams.

Chapter 7: Best Practices for Scalable TypeScript Applications

TypeScript, with its static typing and rich tooling, offers numerous advantages in building scalable applications. In this chapter, we will explore essential best practices for developing scalable TypeScript applications, focusing on code organization, type safety, performance optimization, and team collaboration.

1. Organize Your Codebase

One of the first steps in building scalable applications is to maintain a well-organized codebase. A structured file organization helps developers quickly navigate the project, understand its structure, and locate files easily.

1.1 Feature-Based Structure

Consider organizing your codebase by feature instead of by type (e.g., components, services, models). This structure enhances cohesion and makes it easier to manage code related to specific functionalities.

Example Structure:

```
/src
/features
/auth Auth.tsx authSlice.ts authAPI.ts
/dashboard        Dashboard.tsx        dashboardSlice.ts
dashboardAPI.ts
/common
/components Button.tsx Modal.tsx
```

/hooks useFetch.ts

```
```

1.2 Avoid Deep Nesting

While organizing code, avoid deep nesting of folders that complicates the directory structure. Aim for a balance between organizing your files logically and keeping paths manageable.

1.3 Consistent Naming Conventions

Implement consistent naming conventions for files, classes, and variables. This practice helps improve readability and makes it easier to understand the role of each component in the application.

2. Leverage Type Safety

TypeScript is all about type safety, which can enhance the robustness of your code. Utilize TypeScript's type system to its full potential to avoid runtime errors and make your codebase self-documenting.

2.1 Use Interfaces and Types

Define interfaces and types for function arguments, return values, and data structures. This practice clarifies how different parts of your application interact.

Example:

```typescript
typescript interface User { id: string; name: string; email: string;
}
function getUser(id: string): Promise<User> {
// Implementation
```

```
}
```

2.2 Utilize Enums

For fixed sets of related constants, use TypeScript enums rather than strings or numbers. This enhances type safety and self-documentation.

Example:

```typescript
enum UserRole{

Admin = "ADMIN", User = "USER", Guest = "GUEST",

}
```

2.3 Avoid Using `any`

Avoid using the `any` type as it undermines the core benefits of TypeScript. Instead, use more specific types or generics to maintain type safety.

3. Adhere to SOLID Principles

The SOLID principles are foundational to building scalable applications. These principles promote clean architecture and maintainable code.

3.1 Single Responsibility Principle (SRP)

Each module or class should have one reason to change. Ensure that a component or service encapsulates a single piece of functionality.

3.2 Open/Closed Principle (OCP)

Design your classes and modules to be open for extension but closed for modification. This is often achieved through interfaces and abstract classes.

3.3 Dependency Inversion Principle (DIP)

High-level modules should not depend on low-level modules. Both should depend on abstractions. This can be accomplished through dependency injection, which fosters testability and flexibility.

4. Optimize Performance

Performance is critical for scalability. TypeScript-related optimizations can lead to faster applications and better user experiences.

4.1 Minimize Re-renders

In React applications, use `React.memo` and the `useCallback` and `useMemo` hooks to prevent unnecessary re-renders that can slow down the application.

```typescript
const MemoizedComponent = React.memo(({ value }) =>
{
// Implementation
});
```

4.2 Split Code

Leverage dynamic imports to split code and load only what is necessary for the initial render. This reduces bundle size and enhances load times.

```typescript
```

```
const    LazyComponent    =    React.lazy(()    =>
import('./LazyComponent'));
```
` ` `

4.3 Use Efficient Data Structures

Choosing appropriate data structures can significantly impact performance. Use arrays, sets, maps, and objects judiciously based on the use case to optimize performance.

5. Implement Testing Strategy

A comprehensive testing strategy is essential for maintaining a scalable application. ### 5.1 Type-safe Tests

Take advantage of TypeScript's type system in your test files. This will help catch errors early in the development process.

5.2 Use Testing Frameworks

Utilize popular testing frameworks like Jest or Mocha, along with libraries like React Testing Library, for effective unit and integration testing.

5.3 Write Clear and Concise Tests

Focus on writing tests that are easy to read and understand. Maintain clear separation between unit tests, integration tests, and end-to-end tests.

6. Foster Team Collaboration

Finally, promoting collaboration among team members is key to maintaining a scalable application. Regular code reviews and proper documentation streamline this process.

6.1 Code Reviews

Establish a consistent code review process that emphasizes adhering to best practices and provides constructive feedback.

6.2 Documentation

Maintain thorough documentation using tools like TypeDoc or JSDoc for code comments. A well-documented codebase facilitates onboarding and knowledge sharing among team members.

By adhering to these principles, developers can create applications that are not only powerful and robust but also maintainable and easy to understand. As you advance in your TypeScript journey, remember that good practices contribute significantly to the long-term success of your projects, ultimately leading to happier users and a more productive development team.

Writing Maintainable and Readable TypeScript Code

With time, codebases evolve, team members change, and requirements shift, necessitating a code structure that is easy to understand, adapt, and extend. TypeScript, as a strict syntactical superset of JavaScript, provides several features and best practices that can enhance the readability and maintainability of your code. This chapter explores various strategies, principles, and practical techniques to achieve maintainable and readable TypeScript code.

1. Understand TypeScript Basics

Before diving into best practices, it is crucial to have a solid understanding of TypeScript's basic concepts, such as types, interfaces, and generics. Utilizing the type system effectively can prevent numerous runtime errors and make code self-documenting.

1.1 Type Annotations

Type annotations allow developers to explicitly define the types of variables, function parameters, and return values. This enhances the readability of the code and serves as documentation for anyone reading it later.

```typescript
function add(a: number, b: number): number { return a + b;
}
```

1.2 Interfaces and Types

Using interfaces and type aliases can help describe complex data structures and make your code more organized. This system allows for better code modularity and promotes consistency across your application.

```typescript
interface User {
id: number; name: string;
}
```

```
const user: User = { id: 1,
name: "John Doe"
};
```

2. Employ Proper Naming Conventions

Descriptive and well-thought-out naming conventions greatly increase the readability of code. Invest time in crafting meaningful names for variables, functions, and classes.

2.1 Use Meaningful Names

Choose names that convey purpose. For instance, prefer `calculateTotalPrice` over `ctp`. In addition, naming should reflect the nature and type of the data. For example:

```typescript
const userList: User[] = [];
```

2.2 Consistent Naming Style

Adopt a consistent naming style across your codebase. This could involve using camelCase for variables and functions, PascalCase for classes and types, and UPPER_SNAKE_CASE for constants.

3. Organize Your Code Effectively

Structuring your code correctly helps in maintaining and extending it in the future. ### 3.1 Modular Design

Break down your applications into smaller, self-contained

modules. Each module should have a specific responsibility and be easily testable independently.

```typescript
// user.ts
export interface User { id: number;
name: string;
}
// userService.ts
import { User } from './user';
const getUserById = (id: number): User => {
// implementation
};
```

3.2 File and Directory Structure

Organize files logically, grouping related functionalities together. For instance, you could have a directory structure that separates services, components, and utilities.

```
/src
/components
/services
/models
/utils
```

```
```

4. Write Clear and Concise Code

Simplicity should be a guiding principle in code writing. Clear and concise code is easier to read and understand.

4.1 Avoid Complex Logic

Complex logic can lead to confusion. Where possible, break down complex operations into smaller, well- named functions. This enhances both readability and testability.

```typescript
const calculateDiscount = (price: number, discountRate: number) => { return price - (price * discountRate);
}
```

4.2 Leverage TypeScript Features

Utilize TypeScript's powerful advanced features like generics, union types, and intersection types to create more flexible and reusable components without compromising readability.

```typescript
function identity<T>(arg: T): T { return arg;
}
```

5. Documentation and Comments

Well-documented code is easier to maintain, as it clarifies the purpose and functionality of different parts of your application.

5.1 Use JSDoc Annotations

Employ JSDoc comments to annotate your functions and classes. This provides valuable context and can be automatically used to generate documentation.

```typescript
/**
Adds two numbers together.

@param a - The first number.

@param b - The second number.

@returns The sum of the two numbers.
*/
function add(a: number, b: number): number { return a + b;
}
```

5.2 Comment Wisely

While code should be self-explanatory as much as possible, there are times when comments are necessary. Avoid obvious comments and focus on clarifying complex logic or decisions made in your code.

6. Testing and Quality Assurance

Testing is an essential part of writing maintainable code. A well-tested codebase is easier to refactor and extend.

6.1 Write Unit Tests

Create unit tests for your functions and classes. TypeScript works seamlessly with testing frameworks like Jest and Mocha.

```typescript
test('adds 1 + 2 to equal 3', () => { expect(add(1, 2)).toBe(3);

});
```

6.2 Continuous Integration

Incorporate continuous integration (CI) practices to automatically run tests when changes are made. This reduces the chances of introducing bugs when modifying or adding features.

By following the principles and practices outlined in this chapter, developers can create a robust and adaptable TypeScript codebase that stands the test of time. As your application grows and evolves, these best practices will facilitate the ongoing maintenance and enhancement of your code, leading to greater collaboration and productivity within your team.

Enforcing Best Practices with Linters, Formatters, and TSLint/ESLint

This chapter explores the importance of these tools, focusing on TSLint and ESLint, alongside the benefits of integration into a TypeScript web development workflow. We will provide best practices for setting up and using these tools effectively in your projects, ensuring that your codebase remains consistent and error- free.

1. The Need for Linters and Formatters

As applications grow, so too does the complexity of the code. Linters and formatters help teams adhere to a consistent coding style and reduce errors caused by typos and misconfigurations. Here are a few key reasons why you should leverage these tools:

Consistency: Establishes a common coding style across the team, making the codebase easier to read and maintain.

Error Detection: Catches potential bugs and anti-patterns before code goes into production, reducing the number of issues experienced by users.

Automated Code Review: Reduces the burden on developers by automating parts of the code review process.

Learning Tool: New developers can learn about best practices by observing the recommendations provided by linters.

2. Introducing TSLint and ESLint ### 2.1 TSLint

TSLint was the original linter for TypeScript, designed specifically to support the language's unique features. It provided a wealth of rules to enforce best practices tailored to TypeScript's type system. However, as the web development landscape evolved, the TSLint team announced the deprecation of TSLint in favor of ESLint.

2.2 ESLint

ESLint is a powerful, flexible linter for JavaScript that has become the standard in the industry. With its ability to support TypeScript through plugins, ESLint has positioned itself as the go-to solution for managing code quality in TypeScript projects. The flexibility and community support behind ESLint have made the transition from TSLint smooth and worthwhile.

3. Installing and Configuring ESLint for TypeScript
3.1 Installation

To get started with ESLint in a TypeScript project, you will need to install several packages. Use npm or yarn to add them to your project:

```bash
npm install --save-dev eslint eslint-plugin-import @typescript-eslint/parser @typescript-eslint/eslint-plugin
```

3.2 Configuration

ESLint relies on configuration files to set up its rules and environment. Create an `.eslintrc.js` file in the root of your project and configure it for TypeScript:

```javascript
module.exports = {
parser: '@typescript-eslint/parser', extends: [
'eslint:recommended', 'plugin:@typescript-eslint/recommended',
],
parserOptions: { ecmaVersion: 2020, sourceType: 'module',
},
rules: {
```

119

```
// Custom rules can be defined here
},
};
```

This basic configuration sets up ESLint to utilize the TypeScript parser and recommended settings, ensuring that it understands your TypeScript files.

4. Integrating Prettier for Code Formatting

While ESLint focuses on linting and enforcing code quality, Prettier is a code formatter that ensures a consistent style throughout your files. To set up Prettier alongside ESLint, follow these steps:

4.1 Installation

Install Prettier and its ESLint configuration:

```bash
npm install --save-dev prettier eslint-config-prettier eslint-plugin-prettier
```

4.2 Configuration

Add Prettier to your ESLint configuration to avoid conflicts:

```javascript
module.exports = {
// ... previous config extends: [
// ... other configs 'plugin:prettier/recommended',
],
```

```
rules: {
// Custom ESLint rules
},
};
```

You may also want to create a `.prettierrc` file to configure Prettier settings:

```json
{
"singleQuote": true, "trailingComma": "all"
}
```

5. Automated Linting and Formatting ### 5.1 NPM Scripts

To streamline the linting and formatting processes, consider adding scripts to your `package.json`:

```json "scripts": {
"lint": "eslint. --ext .ts,.tsx", "format": "prettier --write ."
}
```

Now you can easily run linting and formatting from the command line, making it an integral part of your development workflow.

5.2 Pre-commit Hooks

Implementing pre-commit hooks can improve your code

quality by ensuring that code is linted and formatted before it is committed. Tools like Husky and lint-staged can help with this:

```bash
npm install --save-dev husky lint-staged
```

Then, configure Husky in your `package.json`:

```json
"husky": {
"hooks": {
"pre-commit": "lint-staged"
}
},
"lint-staged": {
"*.ts": [
"eslint --fix", "prettier --write", "git add"
]
}
```

By adopting ESLint and Prettier, developers can ensure consistency, catch errors early, and foster a better collaborative environment. Setting up and integrating these tools into your workflow not only saves time but also promotes learning and adherence to industry standards.

Chapter 8: Debugging and Testing TypeScript Code

TypeScript enhances JavaScript by providing static types, interfaces, and a rich ecosystem of tools for building large-scale applications. However, writing TypeScript code also comes with its challenges, making debugging and testing essential.

In this chapter, we will explore effective strategies for debugging TypeScript code, tools that can help streamline the debugging process, and best practices for writing tests in TypeScript applications.

8.1 Debugging TypeScript Code

8.1.1 Understanding Common Errors

Debugging starts with understanding common errors in TypeScript. These include:

Type Errors: TypeScript's type system can catch many errors at compile time, preventing runtime issues. However, type assertion misuses, incorrect types, and null reference errors can still occur.

Syntax Errors: TypeScript extends JavaScript, but it also introduces new syntax. Pay attention to the configuration of your TypeScript compiler to avoid common syntax issues.

Logical Errors: These bugs arise when the code runs without error but does not produce the expected result. Identifying these often requires examining the logic flow.

8.1.2 Using a Debugger

Modern IDEs like Visual Studio Code come equipped with

robust debugging features. Here's how to effectively use a debugger:

Set Breakpoints: Place breakpoints in your code by clicking on the left margin next to the line number. This enables you to pause execution at specific points.

Inspect Variables: When execution is paused at a breakpoint, you can inspect variables in the current scope, allowing you to trace and verify their values.

Step Through Code: Use step-over, step-into, and step-out features to navigate through your code. This lets you follow the execution flow and understand how your code reaches a particular state.

Watch Expressions: Add variables or expressions to the watch list to track their values as you step through the code.

8.1.3 Console Logging

While using a debugger is effective, sometimes quick console logging can provide insights:

```typescript
function calculateTotal(items: number[]): number { let total = 0;

items.forEach(item => { total += item;
```

```
console.log(`Added ${item}, total now is ${total}`);
});
return total;
}
```

While it's not a substitute for robust debugging practices, console logging can help track the flow of data. ### 8.1.4 Leveraging Source Maps

Source maps improve the debugging of TypeScript code by mapping compiled JavaScript back to the original TypeScript source. Ensure your TypeScript compiler configuration (tsconfig.json) has source maps enabled:

```json
{
"compilerOptions": { "sourceMap": true
}
}
```

8.1.5 Tools for Debugging

Aside from built-in IDE debuggers, there are other tools that may assist, such as:

Node.js Inspector: Provides an interactive debugging session for Node.js applications.

Chrome DevTools: For debugging TypeScript code running in the browser. ## 8.2 Testing TypeScript Code

Good testing practices help improve code reliability and

facilitate easier debugging. ### 8.2.1 Choosing a Testing Framework

Several testing frameworks support TypeScript, including:

Jasmine: A behavior-driven development framework for testing JavaScript. It has excellent TypeScript support.

Mocha: A flexible framework that works well with assertion libraries like Chai for behavior verification.

Jest: A popular testing framework that comes with built-in support for TypeScript, making it easy to get started.

8.2.2 Writing Tests

When writing tests in TypeScript, consider the following:

Arrange, Act, Assert: Structure your tests by setting up the context (Arrange), executing the code (Act), and verifying the outcome (Assert).

Types for Mocks and Stubs: When using mocks or stubs, leverage TypeScript's type system to create accurate representations. For example, if you are mocking an API call:

```typescript
interface ApiResponse { data: string[];
}

const mockApiResponse: ApiResponse = { data: ['item1', 'item2']
};
```

Testing Asynchronous Code: Use async/await in your tests to handle Promises seamlessly. Both Jest and Mocha provide excellent support for testing asynchronous code.

```typescript
it('fetches data successfully', async () => { const data = await fetchData(); expect(data).toEqual(['item1', 'item2']);
});
```

8.2.3 Running Tests

Ensure that your tests are set up to run smoothly:

Use a test runner to execute your tests. Tools like Jest come with a built-in runner, while Mocha requires integration with a runner like Karma.

Configure TypeScript to compile tests correctly, ensuring tsconfig.json targets your test files. ### 8.2.4 Continuous Integration

Integrating continuous testing into your development workflow helps detect issues early. Use tools like GitHub Actions, Travis CI, or CircleCI to automate testing every time you push new code.

8.3 Best Practices for Debugging and Testing

Write Type-Safe Code: Leveraging TypeScript's type system can prevent many errors upfront.

Keep Tests Small and Focused: Each test should validate a single behavior or outcome. This makes tests easier to understand and maintain.

Document Your Tests: Comments and descriptive

names help convey the purpose of tests, making life easier for future developers (including yourself).

Refactor Regularly: Don't hesitate to refactor your code for clarity and maintainability. Make sure to change tests accordingly.

Explore Coverage Reports: Use coverage tools that integrate with your testing framework to examine which parts of your code are untested and need attention.

By understanding the common pitfalls you might encounter, utilizing modern debugging techniques, and adopting robust testing practices, you're well on your way to writing reliable TypeScript applications.

Debugging TypeScript with Source Maps and IDE Tools

However, with the right tools and techniques, debugging can become a more manageable and efficient part of your development process. This chapter will explore how to leverage source maps and Integrated Development Environment (IDE) tools to improve your TypeScript debugging experience.

Understanding TypeScript and Source Maps

TypeScript is a superset of JavaScript that offers optional static typing, making it an excellent choice for large-scale web applications. However, when TypeScript code is compiled to JavaScript, it can sometimes become challenging to trace back errors and inspect the original code that triggered them. This is where source maps come into play.

What Are Source Maps?

Source maps are files that map your compiled JavaScript code back to the original TypeScript source code. They serve as a bridge between the minified or transpiled code (which browsers run) and your human- readable TypeScript code. When a browser encounters an error or when you use debugging tools, the source maps allow you to see the original TypeScript code, making it significantly easier to identify and resolve issues.

To enable source maps in your TypeScript project, you need to configure your `tsconfig.json` file. Set the

`sourceMap` option to `true`:

```json
{
"compilerOptions": { "sourceMap": true,

...

}
}
```

Once enabled, the TypeScript compiler generates `.map` files alongside your compiled JavaScript, providing the necessary references for debugging.

Setting Up Your Development Environment

An effective debugging experience begins with the right development environment. Most modern IDEs support TypeScript natively and provide tools that facilitate debugging. Popular choices include Visual Studio Code,

WebStorm, and Atom.

Visual Studio Code (VS Code)

Visual Studio Code is one of the most widely used editors in the TypeScript community due to its robust feature set and extensions. Here's how to set up VS Code for TypeScript debugging:

Install the TypeScript Compiler: Ensure TypeScript is installed or set up in your project. You can install TypeScript globally using npm:

```bash
npm install -g typescript
```

Create a Debug Configuration: Open the Debug view (Ctrl + Shift + D) and create a new launch configuration (`launch.json`). For a typical web app, you might set it up like this:

```json
{
"version": "0.2.0", "configurations": [
{
"type": "chrome",
"request": "launch",
"name": "Launch Chrome against localhost", "url": "http://localhost:3000",
"webRoot": "${workspaceFolder}/src", "sourceMaps":
```

true

}

]

}

```

**Run the TypeScript Compiler**: Start the TypeScript compiler in watch mode to keep your output files up-to-date as you develop:

```bash

tsc --watch

```

Debugging: With your server running (e.g., with `npm start`), use the Debug view to launch Chrome. You can set breakpoints directly in your TypeScript files. As you hit the breakpoints, you'll be able to inspect the current state of the application, including variables, call stacks, and scopes.

WebStorm

WebStorm is another powerful IDE tailored for JavaScript and TypeScript development. The debugging process in WebStorm is straightforward:

Create Node.js Debug Configuration: WebStorm automatically detects TypeScript projects. You can create a new debug configuration through the Run menu.

Enable Source Maps: In the Build, Execution, Deployment settings under TypeScript, ensure that "Generate source maps" is checked.
```

Set Breakpoints and Start Debugging: You can set breakpoints in the TypeScript code, much like in VS Code. Then, run the debug configuration, and WebStorm will handle source maps to show you the original code.

Leveraging Debugging Techniques

While source maps and IDE tools significantly simplify the debugging process, understanding debugging techniques will enhance your problem-solving skills.

Using Breakpoints Effectively

Breakpoints allow you to pause execution at specific lines of code. Use them effectively to inspect values, evaluate expressions, and understand the flow of your application. You can also use conditional breakpoints to stop execution only when specific conditions are met.

Console Logging

While IDE debugging tools are powerful, don't overlook the simplicity of console logging. Outputting variable values and application states to the console can provide quick insights. Use `console.log`, `console.error`, and other logging methods to track down issues. ### Stack Traces

When an error occurs, browsers provide stack traces that can help you identify where things went wrong. Familiarize yourself with reading stack traces to locate the specific point of failure in your code. With source maps enabled, these traces will point directly to your TypeScript files.

DevTools

Most modern browsers come with built-in developer tools.

132

The Chrome DevTools and Firefox Developer Edition can inspect and debug your applications. You can view network requests, analyze performance, and profile memory usage—all valuable for identifying issues in your TypeScript applications.

Embracing these practices will elevate your productivity and enable you to produce cleaner, more resilient code. The combination of TypeScript's type system with robust debugging tools lays the foundation for developing high-quality web applications that can withstand the complexities of real-world use cases.

Writing Unit and Integration Tests with Jest and Cypress

Testing is a fundamental aspect of web development, enabling developers to ensure their applications behave as expected and maintain high levels of quality. This chapter will explore writing unit and integration tests using Jest and Cypress in a TypeScript environment, focusing on best practices and effective methodologies.

Section 1: Introduction to Testing

Testing in software development can be broadly categorized into two types: **unit tests** and **integration tests**.

Unit Tests: These tests focus on individual components or functions, verifying that they perform as intended in isolation. Unit tests usually run quickly and cover specific pieces of logic.

Integration Tests: Unlike unit tests, integration tests evaluate the interactions between multiple components or modules. These tests help identify issues related to how units work together.

Both types of testing are essential for maintaining a robust codebase, especially as applications grow in complexity and size.

Section 2: Setting Up Your Environment

Before diving into writing tests, you must set up your development environment. ### Prerequisites

Node.js and **npm** should be installed on your machine.

A **TypeScript** project set up with `tsconfig.json`.

Jest for unit testing and **Cypress** for integration testing. ### Installation

You can create a new project and install Jest and Cypress via npm as follows:

```bash
mkdir my-testing-project cd my-testing-project npm init -y

npm install --save-dev jest ts-jest @types/jest cypress @types/cypress
```

To configure Jest for TypeScript, create a `jest.config.js` file:

```javascript
module.exports = { preset: 'ts-jest',
testEnvironment: 'node',
```

```
};
```

For Cypress, you can initialize it by running:

```bash
npx cypress open
```

This command will set up default Cypress folders and files in your project. ## Section 3: Writing Unit Tests with Jest

Let's write a simple function and a corresponding test. Suppose we have a utility function that adds two numbers:

src/utils.ts

```typescript
export const add = (a: number, b: number): number => {
return a + b;
};
```

Now, let's write a test for this utility function.

tests/utils.test.ts

```typescript
import { add } from '../src/utils';

describe('add function', () => {

it('should return the sum of two numbers', () => {
expect(add(1, 2)).toBe(3);
```

```
expect(add(-1, 1)).toBe(0);
});
});
```

Running Jest Tests

You can run your tests using the following command:

```bash
npx jest
```

Jest will look for files with `.test.ts` or `.test.js` suffixes and execute the tests contained within. ## Section 4: Writing Integration Tests with Cypress

Cypress is a powerful testing framework primarily used for end-to-end testing, which is a type of integration test. Let's set up a simple integration test for a login page.

Creating a Login Form

Suppose you have a basic HTML login form:

public/index.html

```html

<!DOCTYPE html>
<html lang="en">
<head>
<meta charset="UTF-8">
<meta name="viewport" content="width=device-width, initial-scale=1.0">
```

```html
<title>Login Test</title>
</head>
<body>
<form id="loginForm">
<input                type="text"              id="username"
placeholder="Username" />
<input              type="password"              id="password"
placeholder="Password" />
<button type="submit">Login</button>
</form>
</body>
</html>
```

Writing a Cypress Test Create a new test file for Cypress:

cypress/integration/login.spec.ts

```typescript
describe('Login Page', () => { beforeEach(() => {

cy.visit('http://localhost:3000');      //     Adjust     port
accordingly
});
it('should log in with valid credentials', () => {
cy.get('#username').type('testuser');
cy.get('#password').type('password');
cy.get('#loginForm').submit();
```

```
// Assuming successful login redirects to a welcome page
cy.url().should('include', '/welcome');
});
});
```

Running Cypress Tests

To run your Cypress tests, open Cypress test runner:

```bash
npx cypress open
```

This command will launch the Cypress GUI where you can run your tests interactively. ## Section 5: Best Practices for Writing Tests

Keep Tests Independent: Ensure that each test case can run independently. This decoupling prevents false positives and negatives due to state from other tests.

Use Descriptive Names: Tests should be easy to understand. Use descriptive names for your test cases and suites for clarity.

Mock Dependencies: For unit tests, mock any external dependencies to keep tests fast and reliable. Jest provides powerful mocking capabilities.

Automate Testing in CI/CD: Integrate your testing suite into your CI/CD pipelines. Running tests automatically for each push helps catch issues early.

Limit Test Scope: Keep your tests focused. Unit tests should check one piece of functionality, while integration tests should check broader interactions.

Regularly Refactor Tests: Just as with the application code, regularly review and refactor tests to improve clarity and maintainability.

By following the practices covered in this chapter, you can create a reliable testing suite that minimizes bugs and maximizes quality throughout your development process. Happy testing!

Chapter 9: TypeScript with React: Strongly-Typed Components

This chapter will explore how to harness the power of TypeScript to build strongly-typed components in a React application, making your code more maintainable, readable, and bug-free.

9.1 Introduction to TypeScript and React

TypeScript is a statically typed superset of JavaScript that offers optional type annotations, powerful tooling, and enhanced developer productivity. React, a popular JavaScript library for building user interfaces, can significantly benefit from TypeScript's type system.

By integrating TypeScript into your React project, you can:

Catch errors at compile time rather than at runtime.

Benefit from better autocompletion, navigation, and refactoring capabilities in your IDE.

Define clear interfaces and types for your props and state, enhancing the readability and maintainability of your components.

9.2 Setting Up a TypeScript React Project

To get started, you need a React project configured to use TypeScript. If you are starting from scratch, you can create a new TypeScript React app using Create React App:

```bash
npx create-react-app my-app --template typescript
```

This command sets up a new React application with

TypeScript pre-configured. If you have an existing React project, you can add TypeScript manually by installing the necessary packages:

```bash
npm install --save typescript @types/react @types/react-dom
```

You will also need to rename your files from `.js` to `.tsx` for React components and `.ts` for regular TypeScript files.

9.3 Defining Props and State Types

One of the strengths of TypeScript is its ability to define clear types for component props and state. Let's create a simple component called `UserCard` that displays user information.

Example: UserCard Component First, we define an interface for the props:

```typescript
interface UserCardProps { name: string;
age: number; email: string;
}
```

Next, we create the `UserCard` component:

```tsx
import React from 'react';
const UserCard: React.FC<UserCardProps> = ({ name,
```

```
age, email }) => { return (
<div className="user-card">
<h2>{name}</h2>
<p>Age: {age}</p>
<p>Email: {email}</p>
</div>
);
};
export default UserCard;
```

In this example, we used `React.FC` (a type for functional components) for the `UserCard` component and passed the `UserCardProps` interface to ensure that the component receives the correct types for its props.

9.3.1 Default Props and Optional Props

TypeScript also allows us to define default and optional props. Modify the `UserCardProps` interface as follows:

```typescript
interface UserCardProps { name: string;
age?: number; // optional prop email?: string; // optional prop
}
```

To handle defaults for optional props, you can use default parameter values:

142

```tsx
const UserCard: React.FC<UserCardProps> = ({ name,
age = 0, email = 'N/A',
}) => {
return (
<div className="user-card">
<h2>{name}</h2>
<p>Age: {age}</p>
<p>Email: {email}</p>
</div>
);
};
```

9.4 Working with State

When managing state in your components, you can also define types. Let's create a `UserList` component that maintains a list of users.

Example: UserList Component

```tsx
import React, { useState } from 'react';
interface User { name: string; age: number; email: string;
}
const UserList: React.FC = () => {
const [users, setUsers] = useState<User[]>([
```
143

```tsx
  { name: 'Alice', age: 30, email: 'alice@example.com' },
  { name: 'Bob', age: 25, email: 'bob@example.com' },
]);
return (
<div>
{users.map((user, index) => (
<UserCard key={index} {...user} ></UserCard>
))}
</div>
);
};
export default UserList;
```

In this example, we defined the `User` interface to type the state used in the `UserList` component. By providing a type argument to `useState`, we ensure that the state will always contain an array of objects that adhere to the `User` structure.

9.5 Handling Events in TypeScript

When handling events in React, TypeScript allows you to define the specific event types. Here's how to create a simple form to add a new user using a controlled component.

Example: AddUserForm Component

```tsx
```

```tsx
import React, { useState } from 'react';

const AddUserForm: React.FC<{ onAddUser: (user: User)
=> void }> = ({ onAddUser }) => { const [name, setName]
= useState('');

const [age, setAge] = useState<number | ''>('');

const [email, setEmail] = useState('');

const handleSubmit = (event:
React.FormEvent<HTMLFormElement>) => {
event.preventDefault();

if (name && age !== '' && email) {

onAddUser({ name, age: Number(age), email });
setName('');

setAge('');

setEmail('');

}

};

return (

<form onSubmit={handleSubmit}>

<input value={name} onChange={(e) =>
setName(e.target.value)} placeholder="Name" />

<input type="number" value={age} onChange={(e) =>
setAge(e.target.value)} placeholder="Age" />

<input value={email} onChange={(e) =>
setEmail(e.target.value)} placeholder="Email" />

<button type="submit">Add User</button>

</form>
```

```
);
};
export default AddUserForm;
```

In the `handleSubmit` method, we explicitly typed the event as `React.FormEvent<HTMLFormElement>`. This ensures that TypeScript knows exactly what type of event is being handled, providing better type safety.

9.6 Advanced Types and Generics

TypeScript also offers advanced types and generics, which can be useful in creating more complex components. For instance, if you want to create a generic table component that can display any type of data, you can do so using generics.

Example: Generic Table Component

```tsx
interface TableProps<T> { data: T[];

renderRow: (item: T) => React.ReactNode;

}
function Table<T>({ data, renderRow }: TableProps<T>): JSX.Element { return (

<table>

<tbody>

{data.map((item, index) => (

<tr key={index}>{renderRow(item)}</tr>

))}
```

```
</tbody>
</table>
);
}
```
```

Here, the `Table` component is defined with a generic type parameter `T`, allowing you to specify the type of the data being passed in. The `renderRow` prop is a function that describes how to render each row based on the type of data.

We covered defining props and state types, handling events, creating generic components, and managing defaults and optional props. Harnessing the power of TypeScript in your React applications not only improves code quality but also makes your development experience more enjoyable.

## Using TypeScript with React: Props, State, and Hooks

TypeScript, a superset of JavaScript, provides strong typing that complements the dynamic nature of React applications. In this chapter, we will explore how to effectively integrate TypeScript with React, focusing on Props, State, and the use of Hooks. We will cover essential types and provide practical examples that demonstrate best practices.

## 1. Setting Up TypeScript with React

Before we dive into specifics, let's ensure that we have the
```

right setup. If you're starting a new React project, you can create one that includes TypeScript right from the beginning:

```bash
npx create-react-app my-app --template typescript
```

This command initializes a React application with TypeScript configured. If you have an existing project, you can install TypeScript and the necessary typing definitions:

```bash
npm install --save typescript @types/react @types/react-dom
```

Once your environment is set up, you'll notice that your files will have a `.tsx` extension, allowing you to write JSX in TypeScript.

2. Understanding Props with TypeScript

Props, short for properties, are how data is passed from parent to child components in React. TypeScript allows us to define explicit types for these props, which can help catch errors at compile time rather than run time.

Defining Props Types

To define the type for props in a functional component, we can use an interface:

```tsx
import React from 'react';
```

```tsx
interface GreetingProps { name: string;
age?: number; // age is optional
}
const Greeting: React.FC<GreetingProps> = ({ name, age
}) => { return (
<div>
<h1>Hello, {name}!</h1>
{age && <p>You are {age} years old.</p>}

</div>
);
};
export default Greeting;
```

In this example, the `Greeting` component expects a `name` prop of type `string` and an optional `age` prop of type `number`. Using the `React.FC` generic type further signifies that our component is a functional component.

Default Props

If you want to set default values for props, it can be done with TypeScript as well:

```tsx
Greeting.defaultProps = { age: 25,
};
```

With the above code, if `age` is not provided, it will default to `25`. ## 3. Managing State with TypeScript

State management is another crucial aspect of React applications. When using state in functional components with Hooks, TypeScript helps ensure that the state variables are of the correct type.

Using the `useState` Hook

Here's how to define a state variable with its type:

```tsx
import React, { useState } from 'react';
const Counter: React.FC = () => {
const [count, setCount] = useState<number>(0);
const increment = () => { setCount(count + 1);
};
return (
<div>
<p>Current Count: {count}</p>
<button onClick={increment}>Increment</button>
</div>
);
};
export default Counter;
```

In the `Counter` component, `useState<number>(0)` explicitly declares that `count` will always be a number.

This safeguards against incorrect assignments and keeps our code clean and predictable.

4. Working with Custom Hooks

Custom Hooks are a great way to encapsulate reusable logic in React applications. When defining your own Hook in TypeScript, it's important to specify the return type.

Creating a Custom Hook

Let's create a simple custom hook to manage a boolean state:

```tsx
import { useState } from 'react';

function useToggle(initialValue: boolean = false): [boolean, () => void] { const [value, setValue] = useState<boolean>(initialValue);

const toggle = () => setValue(!value); return [value, toggle];
}
export default useToggle;
```

In this example, the `useToggle` hook manages a boolean state that can be toggled. The return type is specified as a tuple indicating that it returns a boolean and a function.

Using the Custom Hook

Now, we can use our `useToggle` hook in a component:

```tsx
import React from 'react';
```

```tsx
import useToggle from './useToggle';

const ToggleComponent: React.FC = () => { const
[isToggled, toggle] = useToggle();

return (

<div>

<p>The toggle is {isToggled ? 'ON' : 'OFF'}</p>

<button onClick={toggle}>Toggle</button>

</div>

);

};

export default ToggleComponent;
```

This `ToggleComponent` uses `useToggle` to manage its state seamlessly while retaining type safety.

5. TypeScript with Context API

The Context API is another powerful feature for state management, and TypeScript can enhance its usability by ensuring that the right values are being passed around.

Creating a Context

Consider a simple context for a theme:

```tsx
import React, { createContext, useContext, useState } from 'react'; type Theme = "light" | "dark";

interface ThemeContextType { theme: Theme;
```

```
toggleTheme: () => void;

}

const ThemeContext = createContext<ThemeContextType
| undefined>(undefined); export const ThemeProvider:
React.FC = ({ children }) => {

const [theme, setTheme] = useState<Theme>("light");

const toggleTheme = () => {

setTheme((prev) => (prev === "light" ? "dark" : "light"));

};

return (

<ThemeContext.Provider value={{ theme, toggleTheme
}}>

{children}

</ThemeContext.Provider>

);

};

export const useTheme = () => {

const context = useContext(ThemeContext); if (context
=== undefined) {

throw new Error("useTheme must be used within a
ThemeProvider");

}

return context;

};

```
```
```

Consuming Context in a Component

You can now use this context in any component:

```tsx
import React from 'react';

import { useTheme } from './ThemeContext';

const ThemeToggle: React.FC = () => { const { theme, toggleTheme } = useTheme();

return (

<div>

<p>Current Theme: {theme}</p>

<button                    onClick={toggleTheme}>Toggle Theme</button>


</div>

);

};

export default ThemeToggle;
```

By using the techniques covered in this chapter—defining props and state types, creating custom hooks, and utilizing the Context API—you can build maintainable and flexible React applications that scale well over time. As you become comfortable with these concepts, you'll find that TypeScript and React are an incredibly powerful combination.

Advanced React Patterns with TypeScript: Context API and HOCs

This chapter will explore how to leverage the Context API and HOCs effectively while using TypeScript, providing practical examples to illustrate their usage.

Understanding the Context API ### What is the Context API?

The Context API is a React feature that allows you to share values (state, functions, etc.) between components without having to pass them explicitly through props. This is particularly useful when dealing with global data like themes, user authentication, or any state that multiple components might need access to.

Creating a Context

To create a context, you can use the `createContext` function from the React library. Let's start with a simple example where we create a theme context that can hold a dark or light theme.

```typescript
import React, { createContext, useContext, useState, ReactNode } from 'react';

// Define the shape of our context
interface ThemeContextType { theme: string;

toggleTheme: () => void;
}
// Create the context

const ThemeContext = createContext<ThemeContextType
```

```
| undefined>(undefined);

// Define a Provider component

export const ThemeProvider: React.FC<{ children:
ReactNode }> = ({ children }) => { const [theme,
setTheme] = useState<string>('light');

const toggleTheme = () => {

setTheme((prevTheme) => (prevTheme === 'light' ?
'dark' : 'light'));

};

return (

<ThemeContext.Provider value={{ theme, toggleTheme
}}>

{children}

</ThemeContext.Provider>

);

};

// Custom hook to use the Theme Context

export const useTheme = (): ThemeContextType => {
const context = useContext(ThemeContext);

if (!context) {

throw new Error('useTheme must be used within a
ThemeProvider');

}

return context;

};
```

```
```

Using the Context in Components

To use the context in your components, wrap your application with the `ThemeProvider` and use the

`useTheme` hook to access the context values.

```typescript
const App: React.FC = () => { return (
<ThemeProvider>
<ThemeToggle ></ThemeToggle>
<DisplayTheme ></DisplayTheme>
</ThemeProvider>
);
};
const ThemeToggle: React.FC = () => { const { toggleTheme } = useTheme();
return <button onClick={toggleTheme}>Toggle Theme</button>;
};
const DisplayTheme: React.FC = () => { const { theme } = useTheme();
return <div>The current theme is: {theme}</div>;
};
```

Advantages of Using Context with TypeScript

Type Safety: You get the benefits of TypeScript's type-checking, ensuring that your context values maintain their intended types.

Reduced Prop Drilling: Context allows you to avoid passing props through many layers, simplifying component signatures and making your code cleaner and more maintainable.

Scoped State Management: You can localize state management to specific contexts, leading to a more organized codebase.

Exploring Higher-Order Components (HOCs) ### What are Higher-Order Components?

Higher-Order Components (HOCs) are functions that take a component and return a new component, enhancing it with additional functionality. HOCs are a powerful tool for code reusability, allowing you to share logic between different components without duplication.

Creating an HOC

Let's create a simple HOC that injects theme props into a component based on the current theme context we created earlier.

```typescript
import React from 'react';

const withTheme = <P extends object>(

WrappedComponent: React.ComponentType<P & {
theme: string }>

) => {
```

```typescript
return (props: Omit<P, 'theme'>) => { const { theme } =
useTheme();

return    <WrappedComponent    {...(props    as    P)}
theme={theme} ></WrappedComponent>;

};

};
```

Using the HOC

Now you can create themed components using the HOC
by simply wrapping them.

```typescript
const ThemedComponent: React.FC<{ theme: string }> =
({ theme }) => { return <div style={{ background: theme
=== 'dark' ? '#333' : '#FFF' }}> This component is
themed!

</div>;

};

const          EnhancedThemedComponent          =
withTheme(ThemedComponent);
```

Benefits of HOCs

Reusability: Share common logic across multiple
components without repetition.

Separation of Concerns: Keep the logic of data-
fetching, theming, etc., outside of the component so that
the component remains focused on UI rendering.

159

Easy Composition: You can compose multiple HOCs together, creating complex behavior through simple, reusable functions.

Utilizing these patterns in your application not only leads to cleaner and more maintainable code but also leverages TypeScript's strengths to provide a robust development experience. By incorporating these patterns into your development arsenal, you'll be well-equipped to tackle complex React applications with confidence.

Chapter 10: TypeScript with Angular

In this chapter, we'll explore how TypeScript enhances the Angular experience, understand its core features, and see how to harness TypeScript's robustness in building scalable, maintainable web applications.

10.1 What is TypeScript?

TypeScript is a strongly typed programming language that builds on JavaScript by adding optional static types. It was developed by Microsoft and has gained immense popularity among developers because of its ability to catch errors at compile time rather than runtime. This early error detection helps in building safer and more maintainable code.

Key Features of TypeScript:

Static Typing: TypeScript allows you to define variable types, function return types, and complex data structures.

Interfaces: You can define custom types and enforce contracts within your application, making the code more predictable.

Classes: TypeScript offers support for object-oriented programming, including class inheritance, encapsulation, and polymorphism.

Modules: TypeScript supports modular programming, making it easier to manage code and dependencies.

Tooling: TypeScript integrates seamlessly with IDEs and text editors, providing features like autocompletion, type checking, and refactoring tools.

10.2 Angular and TypeScript: A Perfect Match

Angular was designed with TypeScript in mind. By leveraging TypeScript, Angular developers can enjoy enhanced code quality and improved development efficiency. Let's look at how TypeScript fits into the Angular ecosystem.

Benefits of Using TypeScript in Angular:

Enhanced Readability: Type annotations make the code self-documenting, which improves readability and maintainability.

Type Inference: With TypeScript's type inference, developers can write less boilerplate code while still benefiting from type safety.

Rich IDE Support: TypeScript offers powerful tooling support, including intelligent code completion and real-time error detection, which boosts developer productivity.

Large Community and Ecosystem: The combination of Angular and TypeScript has a large and active community, offering a wealth of resources, libraries, and best practices.

10.3 Setting Up an Angular Project with TypeScript

To start building an Angular application using TypeScript, you need to set up a development environment. Angular CLI (Command Line Interface) simplifies the process of creating and managing Angular projects.

Step 1: Install Angular CLI

First, ensure that you have Node.js installed. Then, install the Angular CLI globally using npm:

```bash
```

```bash
npm install -g @angular/cli
```

Step 2: Create a New Angular Project Use the Angular CLI to create a new project:

```bash
ng new my-angular-app
```

This command will prompt you to choose `routing` and the stylesheet format you want to use (CSS, SCSS, etc.). Once completed, navigate into your project folder:

```bash
cd my-angular-app
```

Step 3: Verify TypeScript Configuration

By default, Angular CLI projects come with TypeScript configured. You can check the `tsconfig.json` file in your project root, which contains the TypeScript compiler options.

10.4 Writing Angular Components with TypeScript

In Angular, components are the building blocks of your application. Let's walk through creating a simple component using TypeScript.

Creating a Component

Generate a new component using Angular CLI:

```bash
ng generate component my-component
```

```
` ` `
```

This command creates a new folder `my-component` with the necessary files. Open `my- component.component.ts ` to see how TypeScript is used:

```typescript
import { Component } from '@angular/core';

@Component({
selector: 'app-my-component',
templateUrl:          './my-component.component.html',
styleUrls: ['./my-component.component.css']
})

export class MyComponent { title: string;

constructor() {

this.title = 'Welcome to My Component!';

}

}
```

TypeScript Features in Components

In this component, we have defined a property `title` with a type annotation `string`. This levels up our TypeScript usage:

Constructor: We initialized the `title` property in the constructor, showcasing TypeScript's constructor syntax.

Type Safety: If we accidentally assign a different type

to `title`, TypeScript will throw a compile-time error, aiding in early error detection.

10.5 Advanced TypeScript Features in Angular

As projects grow, leveraging more advanced TypeScript features can lead to even more robust applications. ### Interfaces and Type Aliases

Using interfaces in TypeScript can help you define complex data structures. Consider a user object:

```typescript
export interface User { id: number;

name: string; email: string;

}
```

You can then use this interface in your components or services:

```typescript
import { Component } from '@angular/core'; import {
User } from './user.interface';

@Component({ selector: 'app-user-list',

template: '<div *ngFor="let user of users">{{ user.name }}</div>',

})
export class UserListComponent { users: User[] = [

{ id: 1, name: 'Alice', email: 'alice@example.com' },

{ id: 2, name: 'Bob', email: 'bob@example.com' },
```

```
];
}
```

Enums for Better Code Management

Enums can also be extremely useful in Angular applications:

```typescript
export enum UserRole { Admin = 'ADMIN', User = 'USER',

Guest = 'GUEST',

}
```

Using enums helps in making your codebase cleaner and avoiding 'magic strings'. ## 10.6 Error Handling with TypeScript

TypeScript brings better error handling techniques by allowing you to define the type of errors you expect. You can enhance service responses by throwing appropriate types of errors:

```typescript
import { Injectable } from '@angular/core';

import { HttpClient, HttpErrorResponse } from '@angular/common/http'; import { Observable, throwError } from 'rxjs';

import { catchError } from 'rxjs/operators';
```

```
@Injectable({ providedIn: 'root',
})
export class DataService {
private    apiUrl    =    'https://api.example.com/data';
constructor(private http: HttpClient) {}
getData(): Observable<Data[]> {
return          this.http.get<Data[]>(this.apiUrl).pipe(
catchError(this.handleError)
);
}
handleError(error:        HttpErrorResponse)        {
console.error('An error occurred:', error.message);
return throwError('Something went wrong; please try
again later.');
}
}
```
```

In this example, the `handleError` method provides a strong typing mechanism around error handling, making it clear to other developers what types of responses can be handled.

## 10.7 Best Practices for Using TypeScript with Angular

To get the most out of TypeScript in your Angular applications, consider the following best practices:

**Use Explicit Types**: Always define types for your properties, function parameters, and return values.
```

Leverage Interfaces: Use interfaces to create contracts and document the shape of data structures used in your application.

Utilize Enums: Replace strings with enums for state management and fixed sets of constants.

Keep Your Code DRY (Don't Repeat Yourself): Reuse interfaces and types across components to avoid redundancy.

The integration of TypeScript not only enhances the development experience but also leads to robust and maintainable code. Understanding these principles allows developers to harness the full potential of Angular, creating applications that are not only performant but also easier to scale and maintain.

Leveraging TypeScript in Angular Applications

One of the key components that sets Angular apart is its seamless integration with TypeScript, a superset of JavaScript that brings strong typing, advanced tooling, and scalable architecture to the development process. This chapter explores how to effectively leverage TypeScript in Angular applications to enhance code quality, improve maintainability, and streamline developer productivity.

Understanding TypeScript and Its Benefits

TypeScript was developed by Microsoft to address the complexities that arise from growing JavaScript applications. It introduces static typing, interfaces, classes, and other modern programming constructs, which can make the development process more robust and organized. Some key benefits of using TypeScript in

Angular applications include:

Static Typing: TypeScript allows developers to define types for variables, function parameters, and return values. This helps catch errors at compile-time rather than runtime, significantly reducing the potential for bugs.

Enhanced Tooling: TypeScript's static type system provides rich IDE support, including code completion, refactoring capabilities, and easier navigation. This boosts developer productivity and helps maintain a cleaner codebase.

Improved Code Readability: By using interfaces and explicit type definitions, developers can create clearer APIs and data structures, making it easier for teams to work collaboratively and recognize data flow at a glance.

Embracing Modern JavaScript Features: TypeScript supports modern JavaScript features and provides backward compatibility, allowing developers to use new syntax and features while still targeting older browsers.

Easier Refactoring: With TypeScript's static typing, refactoring becomes less hazardous. Developers can confidently make changes knowing that the type system will catch inconsistencies and errors.

Setting Up TypeScript in an Angular Application

To begin leveraging TypeScript in an Angular application, you typically start a new Angular project using Angular CLI, which comes with TypeScript configured out of the box. Here's how you can initiate a new Angular project:

```bash
ng new my-angular-app cd my-angular-app
```

ng serve
` ` `

This command sets up the project structure, installs the necessary dependencies, and makes TypeScript ready for use. You'll find a file called `tsconfig.json`, which serves as the configuration file for TypeScript. This file allows developers to specify compiler options like strictness, module resolution, and target ECMAScript version.

TypeScript Features in Angular

1. Classes and Interfaces

Angular heavily relies on classes to define components, services, and other constructs. TypeScript enhances this by allowing the definition of interfaces that can enforce structure on objects. For example:

```typescript
export interface User { id: number;

name: string; email: string;

}

export class UserService { private users: User[] = [];

constructor() { }

addUser(user: User): void { this.users.push(user);

}

getUsers(): User[] { return this.users;

}

}
```

```
```

In this example, we define a `User` interface that outlines the structure expected of a user object, ensuring greater consistency in how user data is handled throughout the application.

2. Decorators

Angular employs decorators (e.g., `@Component`, `@Injectable`) to add metadata to classes. With TypeScript, you can create strongly typed decorators that provide additional compile-time checks. For instance:

```typescript
import { Component } from '@angular/core';

@Component({ selector: 'app-user',

templateUrl: './user.component.html',

})

export class UserComponent { user: User;

constructor() {

this.user = { id: 1, name: 'John Doe', email: 'john.doe@example.com' };

}

}
```

3. Type Guards

Type guards are type-checking constructs that help ensure the correct data types are being used in conditional

171

statements. They can be particularly useful for narrowing down types in complex conditional logic:

```typescript
function isUser(user: any): user is User {

return user && typeof user.id === 'number' && typeof user.name === 'string';

}

let user: any = getSomeUser(); if (isUser(user)) {

console.log(user.name); // Safe to access user.name

}
```

4. Generics

TypeScript's generics enable developers to create reusable components and services while preserving the type information. This is especially useful for services that manage collections of similar types:

```typescript
@Injectable({ providedIn: 'root',

})

export class DataService<T> { private items: T[] = [];

addItem(item: T): void { this.items.push(item);

}

getItems(): T[] { return this.items;

}

}
```

This generic data service can be used for any type of data, ensuring reusability and type safety. ## Best Practices for Using TypeScript in Angular

Utilize Strict Mode: Enable strict mode in your `tsconfig.json` file to enforce strict type-checking options. This can help catch potential issues early in development.

Define Interfaces: Use interfaces to define the shape of complex objects, especially for API responses. This promotes consistency and better type inference.

Leverage Enums: When dealing with sets of related constants, utilize TypeScript's enums to improve code clarity and maintainability.

Write Type-safe Services and Components: Always type your services and component properties, especially when dealing with external data sources, to ensure consistency throughout your application.

Use Utility Types: Familiarize yourself with TypeScript's utility types (e.g., `Partial<T>`, `Pick<T, K>`, `Record<K, T>`) to manipulate types conveniently while maintaining type safety.

By embracing the features of TypeScript, developers can create applications that are more maintainable, less prone to runtime errors, and ultimately easier to scale. By following best practices and understanding how to harness TypeScript's powerful features, developers can significantly enhance their Angular development experience, leading to faster and more efficient workflows.

Dependency Injection and Strongly-Typed Services

This chapter delves into the core principles of Dependency Injection, the advantages of TypeScript's strong typing system, and practical implementations that empower developers to create robust and responsive web applications.

1. Understanding Dependency Injection ### 1.1 What is Dependency Injection?

Dependency Injection is a design pattern used to manage the dependencies between classes, particularly how they acquire what they need from external sources rather than creating them internally. This promotes loose coupling, where classes are independent of their dependencies' implementations. In simpler terms, DI allows objects to receive their dependencies from an external source rather than creating them themselves.

1.2 Benefits of Dependency Injection

Improved Testability: By decoupling components, you can easily substitute real services with mock services during testing.

Ease of Maintenance: Changes to a service's implementation can be performed without affecting the consumers of that service.

Reusable Components: Components can be reused across different parts of the application without needing to change how dependencies are wired up.

Simplified Configuration: DI frameworks help

manage the creation and binding of dependencies, making it easier to configure services centrally.

1.3 Dependency Injection in Practice

In TypeScript, we can implement Dependency Injection using various approaches—manual DI, constructor injection, and using DI frameworks such as InversifyJS or Angular's built-in DI system. Here's a simple manual approach:

```typescript
// Service Interface interface Logger {

log(message: string): void;

}
// Concrete Implementation

class ConsoleLogger implements Logger { log(message: string): void {

console.log(message);

}

}
// Component that depends on the Logger class UserService {

private logger: Logger;

constructor(logger: Logger) { this.logger = logger;

}

public createUser(username: string): void {

// Logic to create user
```

```typescript
    this.logger.log(`User ${username} created.`);
  }
}

// Main application code
const logger = new ConsoleLogger();

const userService = new UserService(logger);
userService.createUser('Alice');
```

2. Strongly-Typed Services in TypeScript ### 2.1 Why Strong Typing Matters

TypeScript's type system is one of its most powerful features. It allows developers to catch errors early in the development process, create self-documenting code, and enhance tooling support. Strongly-typed services can significantly enhance a web application's robustness by reducing runtime errors.

2.2 Defining Strongly-Typed Services

Strongly-typed services involve creating interfaces or classes that explicitly define the shape of your data and behavior. This not only offers better IntelliSense support but also clarifies the contract for consumers of these services.

```typescript
// Defining a strongly-typed User interface interface User {
  id: number; username: string;
}
```

```typescript
// Service for handling users class UserService {
private users: User[] = [];
public addUser(user: User): void { this.users.push(user);
}
public getUserById(id: number): User | undefined { return
this.users.find(user => user.id === id);
}
}


// Usage example
const userService = new UserService();
userService.addUser({ id: 1, username: 'Alice' }); const
user = userService.getUserById(1); console.log(user);
```

2.3 Utilizing Dependency Injection with Strongly-Typed Services

By combining DI with strongly-typed services, we ensure that our components have well-defined contracts, reducing the likelihood of errors and improving code quality.

```typescript
// Defining the UserRepository interface interface
UserRepository {
addUser(user: User): void;
getUserById(id: number): User | undefined;
}
```

```typescript
// Concrete implementation of UserRepository
class InMemoryUserRepository implements UserRepository { private users: User[] = [];

public addUser(user: User): void { this.users.push(user);
}

public getUserById(id: number): User | undefined { return this.users.find(user => user.id === id);
}
}

// Updating UserService to accept UserRepository class UserService {

constructor(private userRepository: UserRepository) {}

public createUser(username: string): void {

const newUser: User = { id: Date.now(), username }; // Simple logic for ID this.userRepository.addUser(newUser);
}

public findUser(id: number): User | undefined { return this.userRepository.getUserById(id);
}
}

// Main application code
const userRepository = new InMemoryUserRepository();
const userService = new UserService(userRepository);
userService.createUser('Alice');
console.log(userService.findUser(1));
```
```

178
```

Dependency Injection and strongly-typed services in TypeScript represent a harmonious approach to building modern web applications. By embracing these concepts, developers can create systems that are easier to test, maintain, and scale. Furthermore, TypeScript's strong type system helps in building a more predictable and manageable codebase.

In a landscape where complexity is the norm, adopting Dependency Injection and leveraging TypeScript's capabilities empowers developers to focus on delivering high-quality software while minimizing common pitfalls associated with tightly coupled architectures. As web development continues to evolve, these practices will serve as foundational techniques for creating sophisticated applications with confidence.

Additional Resources

[InversifyJS Documentation](https://inversify.io/)

[TypeScript Handbook](https://www.typescriptlang.org/docs/handbook/intro.html)

[Design Patterns in TypeScript](https://refactoring.guru/design-patterns/typescript)

By understanding and applying the concepts discussed in this chapter, developers can navigate the complexities of web development with greater ease, paving the way for innovative and effective applications.

Chapter 11: TypeScript in Full-Stack Web Development

This chapter delves into how TypeScript can be seamlessly integrated into full-stack web development, covering its advantages, architectural patterns, and frameworks that can benefit from TypeScript's features.

1. Understanding TypeScript ### 1.1 What is TypeScript?

TypeScript is a superset of JavaScript that introduces static typing, interfaces, and other features that enhance the language's capabilities. By allowing developers to specify types for variables, function parameters, and return values, TypeScript provides an added layer of type safety that can prevent common programming errors.

1.2 Advantages of TypeScript

Type Safety: Catch errors during development rather than at runtime.

Enhanced Code Readability: Clearer definitions of data structures and variables aid in understanding the codebase.

Better Tooling: IDEs can offer improved autocomplete, code navigation, and refactoring tools, significantly boosting developer productivity.

Interoperability with JavaScript: Existing JavaScript code can be gradually migrated to TypeScript, allowing for a smooth transition.

2. TypeScript in Full-Stack Development

Full-stack development typically involves working with

both the front-end and back-end of an application. TypeScript can improve the developer experience and maintainability across both realms.

2.1 TypeScript on the Front-End

When it comes to front-end development, frameworks like React, Angular, and Vue have embraced TypeScript, allowing developers to write safer and more maintainable code.

2.1.1 React with TypeScript

React's component-based architecture pairs well with TypeScript's type definitions. By using TypeScript with React, developers can define props and state types, making components easier to understand and use.

Example of a simple React component in TypeScript:

```typescript
import React from 'react';

interface MyComponentProps { title: string;

isActive: boolean;

}

const MyComponent: React.FC<MyComponentProps> = ({ title, isActive }) => { return (

<div>

<h1>{title}</h1>

{isActive && <p>The component is active!</p>}

</div>

);
```

```
};
export default MyComponent;
```

2.1.2 Angular with TypeScript

Angular is built from the ground up with TypeScript, promoting strong typing and decorators that enhance the development process. Angular's reliance on TypeScript means that all aspects of the framework, including services, components, and modules, are optimized for a typed environment.

Example of an Angular component:

```typescript
import { Component } from '@angular/core';
@Component({
selector: 'app-hello-world', template: `<h1>{{ title }}</h1>`
})
export class HelloWorldComponent { title: string;
constructor() {
this.title = 'Hello, TypeScript!';
}
}
```

2.2 TypeScript on the Back-End

On the server side, Node.js applications can significantly

benefit from TypeScript's features. Frameworks such as Express.js can be typed, providing enhanced clarity and type safety.

2.2.1 Using TypeScript with Express.js

TypeScript can be utilized to define the structure of request and response objects, improving the robustness of API endpoints.

Example of a simple Express server in TypeScript:

```typescript
import express, { Request, Response } from 'express';

const app = express(); const PORT = 3000;

app.get('/api/example', (req: Request, res: Response) => {
res.json({ message: 'Hello from TypeScript API!' });
});
app.listen(PORT, () => {

console.log(`Server                running              at
http://localhost:${PORT}`);

});
```

3. Building a Full-Stack Application with TypeScript

In this section, we will walk through the steps necessary to create a simple full-stack application using TypeScript.

3.1 Setting Up the Project

Initialize the Project: Create a new directory and initialize npm.

```bash
```

```bash
mkdir ts-fullstack-app cd ts-fullstack-app npm init -y
```

Install Dependencies:

For the front-end (e.g., using React):

```bash
npx create-react-app client --template typescript
```

For the back-end (Node.js with Express):

```bash
mkdir server cd server
```

npm install express

npm install --save-dev typescript @types/node @types/express ts-node

```

### 3.2 Create a Simple API Endpoint

In the `server` folder, create an `index.ts` file and include the Express server code as shown above. ### 3.3 Build the Front-End Application

In the `client` folder, create a simple component to fetch data from the newly created API endpoint.

```typescript
import React, { useEffect, useState } from 'react';

const App: React.FC = () => {

const [message, setMessage] = useState('');
```
```

```
useEffect(() => { fetch('/api/example')
.then((res) => res.json())
.then((data) => setMessage(data.message));
}, []);
return <h1>{message}</h1>;
};
export default App;
```

3.4 Running the Application

Run the Back-End: From the `server` folder, use ts-node to start the server.

```bash
npx ts-node index.ts
```

Run the Front-End: From the `client` folder, start the React application.

```bash npm start
```

4. Advantages of TypeScript in Full-Stack Development

Code Consistency: TypeScript promotes uniformity across both the client and server code, making it easier for developers to switch contexts.

Shared Models: TypeScript allows for the sharing of

interfaces and types between the client and server, ensuring consistency in data structures.

Improved Collaboration: With explicit typing and interfaces, teams can communicate more effectively, reducing misunderstandings about code functionality.

By enhancing both front-end and back-end code with type safety and clearer structure, TypeScript significantly improves the maintainability and scalability of full-stack applications. As web development continues to evolve, embracing TypeScript will allow developers to create more reliable and robust applications that can handle the complexities of modern web requirements.

Sharing Types Between Frontend and Backend for Consistency

In this chapter, we will discuss techniques and best practices for sharing types between the frontend and backend, ensuring that both sides of your application speak the same language.

The Importance of Consistent Types

When working with TypeScript in both the frontend and backend, maintaining consistent types has multiple advantages:

Type Safety: Consistent types help catch errors early in the development process, reducing runtime errors and bugs.

Improved Collaboration: Teams can work together more effectively when they adhere to the same type definitions, improving communication between frontend and backend developers.

Easier Refactoring: When types change, TypeScript can help identify where adjustments are necessary, making it easier to refactor and maintain code.

Enhanced Developer Experience: IDEs and text editors can provide better autocompletion, navigation, and documentation features when types are consistently defined.

Setting Up a Shared Types Directory

To share types between the frontend and backend, a common approach is to create a shared directory where all type definitions reside. This shared structure allows both frontend and backend code to import and use the same type declarations.

Step-by-Step Guide to Creating a Shared Types Directory

Create a Shared Directory: In your project structure, create a `types` directory at the root level or within a dedicated `shared` folder. This can be structured as follows:

```

/project-root

/frontend

/backend

/shared

/types

```

187

Define Types: Inside the `types` directory, create files to define your TypeScript interfaces and types. For instance:

```typescript
// shared/types/User.ts export interface User {

id: number; username: string; email: string; createdAt: Date; updatedAt: Date;

}
```

Update Configuration: Ensure your TypeScript configuration files (tsconfig.json) for both frontend and backend reference the shared directory. You may need to adjust the `include` or `paths` settings to allow TypeScript to resolve these types correctly.

```json
// tsconfig.json for backend

{

"include": ["src", "../shared/types"]

}
```

Import Types: In both your frontend and backend code, you can now import and use the shared types:

```typescript
// frontend/src/components/UserProfile.tsx import { User } from '../../shared/types/User';
```

188

```typescript
const UserProfile: React.FC<{ user: User }> = ({ user })
=> { return <div>{user.username}</div>;
};
```

```typescript
// backend/src/controllers/userController.ts import {
User } from '../../shared/types/User';

const createUser = (userData: User) => {
// handle user creation
};
```

Handling API Request and Response Types

When your frontend and backend communicate over APIs, defining types for request and response bodies becomes crucial. You can extend your shared types to include these definitions.

Example

Define API Types:

```typescript
// shared/types/UserApi.ts
export interface CreateUserRequest { username: string;

email: string;
}
export interface CreateUserResponse { id: number;
```

```typescript
username: string; email: string;
createdAt: Date; updatedAt: Date;
}
```

Use Types in API Calls:

On the frontend, you can use these types to ensure your API calls adhere to the defined structure.

```typescript
// frontend/src/api/userApi.ts
import { CreateUserRequest, CreateUserResponse } from '../../shared/types/UserApi';

const createUser = async (data: CreateUserRequest): Promise<CreateUserResponse> => { const response = await fetch('/api/users', {
method: 'POST',
headers: { 'Content-Type': 'application/json' }, body: JSON.stringify(data),
});
return response.json();
};
```

Use Types in Backend:

Similarly, in your backend, you can use these types when handling requests.

```typescript
```

```
// backend/src/routes/userRoutes.ts

import { CreateUserRequest } from
'../../shared/types/UserApi';

app.post('/api/users', (req, res) => {

const userData: CreateUserRequest = req.body;

// Validate and create user

});
```

Best Practices

Versioning Shared Types: When changes are made to the shared types, consider versioning these types to avoid breaking changes for teams reliant on older versions.

Testing: Ensure that your shared types are covered by tests to verify their integrity. Consider using tools like Jest or Mocha for type testing.

Documentation: Maintain updated documentation on how to use the shared types, including examples and usage guidelines, to ease onboarding for new developers.

Keep It Simple: While sharing types is valuable, avoid creating an overly complex system of types that may lead to confusion. Only share what is necessary.

Use Namespaces If Necessary: For larger applications, consider using namespaces to organize and categorize your types for better readability.

By setting up a shared types directory and defining clear interfaces for your application, you create a robust environment where both frontend and backend code can effectively communicate. As you implement these strategies, remember to prioritize maintainability and clarity in your shared type definitions. The payoff is a more resilient application that is easier to develop, extend, and maintain.

GraphQL with TypeScript: End-to-End Type Safety

Enter GraphQL and TypeScript—two powerful technologies that, when combined, provide an unparalleled experience in building full-stack applications with the kind of type safety that developers have long dreamed of.

In this chapter, we will delve into how GraphQL and TypeScript work together to create a seamless development experience, one that minimizes runtime errors and enhances overall productivity. We will explore the core concepts of GraphQL, the features of TypeScript that lend themselves to type safety, and practical implementation strategies to create a GraphQL API and a client application, all while leveraging TypeScript's capabilities.

Understanding GraphQL

GraphQL, developed by Facebook, is a query language for APIs, and a runtime for executing those queries. Unlike traditional RESTful APIs, which often expose multiple endpoints for different resources, GraphQL allows clients to request precisely the data they need in a single query. This fine-grained control over data fetching can lead to more efficient applications and a better user experience.

The Basics of GraphQL

At its core, GraphQL consists of:

Schema Definition: The schema defines the types and relationships within your API. This is typically done through a `GraphQL schema language` that allows you to specify types, queries, and mutations.

Queries and Mutations: Queries are used to fetch data, while mutations are used for creating, updating, or deleting data. Each operation returns specific types defined in the schema.

Types: GraphQL supports scalar types (like `String`, `Int`, and `Boolean`) and complex types (such as `Object`, `Interface`, and `Union`). Custom types can be defined to suit the needs of your application.

Setting Up a GraphQL Server

To demonstrate the type safety features of TypeScript paired with GraphQL, let's consider setting up a simple GraphQL server. We will use `Apollo Server`, a popular choice for building GraphQL APIs in Node.js.

```bash
npm install apollo-server graphql
```

With Apollo Server, you can define your schema using the Apollo Server API. Below is an example of a simple server that defines a `User` type:

```typescript
import { ApolloServer, gql } from 'apollo-server';

// Define your type definitions using GraphQL schema
language const typeDefs = gql`
type User { id: ID!
name: String! email: String!
}
type Query { users: [User!]!
}
`;
// Define resolvers to fetch data const resolvers = {
Query: { users: () => [
{ id: '1', name: 'John Doe', email: 'john@example.com' },
{ id: '2', name: 'Jane Smith', email: 'jane@example.com' },
],
},
};
// Create an instance of Apollo Server with the type
definitions and resolvers const server = new
ApolloServer({ typeDefs, resolvers });
// Start the server server.listen().then(({ url }) => {
console.log(`???? Server ready at ${url}`);
});
```

194

```
```

Adding TypeScript to the Mix

With our basic GraphQL server in place, let's introduce TypeScript for end-to-end type safety. TypeScript will help catch errors at compile time, allowing developers to understand and predict application behavior more confidently.

Type Definitions in TypeScript

First, we need to define TypeScript types that correlate to our GraphQL schema. This not only provides type safety in our resolver functions but also ensures we maintain consistency between our backend and frontend.

```typescript
type User = { id: string; name: string; email:
string;
};
type Query = { users: User[];
};
```

Ensuring Type Safety in Resolvers

Next, we'll enhance our resolvers with type definitions, ensuring that the data returned is strictly typed and adheres to our defined structure.

```typescript
const resolvers: Resolvers = { Query: {
users: (): User[] => [
{ id: '1', name: 'John Doe', email: 'john@example.com' },
```

```
  { id: '2', name: 'Jane Smith', email: 'jane@example.com' },
  ],
  },
};
```
```

In this example, we use TypeScript interfaces to define the structure of the data being used within our server. This ensures that any modification or usage crisis of our `User` type will be caught at compile time instead of failing at runtime.

## Exploring Type-Safe Clients with GraphQL

Having set up our type-safe GraphQL server, it's time to create a client that interacts with it while maintaining the same level of type safety.

### Using Apollo Client with TypeScript

For our client-side implementation, we can use `Apollo Client`, a powerful library for managing GraphQL data in modern applications. Install it as follows:

```bash
npm install @apollo/client graphql
```

TypeScript Integration with Apollo Client

When querying data with Apollo, we can define TypeScript interfaces. This promotes type safety for GraphQL queries and responses, reducing errors when accessing properties.

```typescript
```
```

```typescript
import { ApolloClient, InMemoryCache, gql, useQuery }
from '@apollo/client';

// Initialize the Apollo Client const client = new
ApolloClient({

uri: 'http://localhost:4000', // Your GraphQL server URL
cache: new InMemoryCache(),

});

// Define GraphQL query const GET_USERS = gql` query
GetUsers {

users { id name


email
}
}
`;

// Define TypeScript interface for the query result
interface UsersData {

users: User[];

}

// Use the query within a component const
UsersComponent = () => {

const { loading, error, data } =
useQuery<UsersData>(GET_USERS);

if (loading) return <p>Loading...</p>;

if (error) return <p>Error: {error.message}</p>;
```

```
return (
<ul>
{data?.users.map(user => (
<li key={user.id}>
{user.name} - {user.email}
</li>
))}
</ul>
);
};
```
` ` `

In the example above, we define our query using the GraphQL syntax and provide a TypeScript interface that reflects the structure of the expected response. This allows for safe data access in our components.

Combining GraphQL with TypeScript leads to an environment where both server and client sides are fully aware of the data they work with, ensuring end-to-end type safety. This integration decreases the likelihood of bugs, simplifies the data-fetching process, and provides developers with a clear contract of how data can be structured and manipulated.

Conclusion

As we reach the end of "TypeScript for Web Development," it's essential to reflect on the journey we've taken together and the transformative power of TypeScript in modern web development. Throughout this book, we've explored how TypeScript enhances productivity, minimizes costly errors, and empowers developers to create scalable web applications with confidence and efficiency.

We began by understanding the fundamental concepts of TypeScript and how it integrates seamlessly with JavaScript, opening the door to a more structured and error-resistant coding experience. By embracing strong typing, developers can catch errors early in the development process, reducing the time spent on debugging and increasing overall project maintainability. This proactive approach not only ensures smoother workflows but also fosters a culture of quality and collaboration within development teams.

We also delved into practical techniques and best practices that elevate TypeScript's capabilities. From leveraging interfaces and enums to utilizing advanced features like generics and decorators, we've seen how TypeScript can accommodate both simple and complex applications. The rich ecosystem of tools and frameworks that support TypeScript, such as Angular, React, and Node.js, further illustrates its versatility and widespread adoption.

As you embark on your TypeScript journey, remember that the primary goal is to build robust, scalable applications that fulfill user needs effectively. The skills and knowledge you've acquired through this book will empower you to tackle challenges with confidence and efficiency, creating solutions that are not only functional but also elegant in their design.

Finally, embrace the TypeScript community. With its vibrant group of developers and resources, you'll find ongoing support and inspiration as you continue to hone your skills and expand your understanding. The landscape of web development is ever-evolving, and staying connected with fellow developers will ensure you remain at the forefront of innovation.

Thank you for joining me on this exploration of TypeScript. I hope this book has equipped you with the tools and insights necessary to enhance your web development capabilities. Here's to building exceptional applications and achieving new heights in your coding journey! Happy coding!

Biography

Adrian is a passionate innovator and a visionary in the world of **Miller**, blending deep expertise with a relentless drive to push boundaries. With a background rooted in **web development, TypeScript programming, and blockchain technology**, Adrian thrives at the intersection of cutting-edge technology and practical applications. His work in **web applications** has empowered countless developers and entrepreneurs to build scalable, high-performance digital solutions.

Beyond his technical prowess, Adrian is fueled by a love for problem-solving and creative innovation. Whether he's architecting blockchain solutions or refining his latest **TypeScript-powered application**, his mission is always the same—to simplify the complex and unlock new possibilities for others.

When he's not coding or writing, you'll find Adrian exploring the ever-evolving landscape of decentralized technology, mentoring aspiring developers, or experimenting with the latest web frameworks. His dedication to learning and sharing knowledge makes his work not just insightful but transformative.

Through this Book, Adrian brings his expertise, passion, and real-world experience to guide readers on their own journey—offering not just knowledge, but a roadmap to success.

Glossary: TypeScript for Web Development

A

Abrstraction

A principle in programming that allows for reducing complexity by hiding implementation details and exposing only the essential features of an object or system. In TypeScript, abstract classes and interfaces are commonly used to achieve abstraction.

Any

A TypeScript type that allows for any value, bypassing the type-checking system. While convenient, it's advisable to use it sparingly to maintain type safety.

B

Base Class

A class that is being extended by one or more subclasses.

In TypeScript, base classes can provide common properties and methods that derived classes can inherit.

Boolean

A fundamental data type in TypeScript that can only have two values: `true` or `false`. ### C

Class

A blueprint for creating objects in TypeScript, defined with properties (attributes) and methods (functions). TypeScript enhances JavaScript classes with additional features like access modifiers and interfaces.

Constructor

A special method within a class that is called when an instance of that class is created. It is typically used to initialize class properties.

D

Decorator

A special type of declaration that can be attached to a class, method, accessor, property, or parameter. Decorators allow for adding metadata or modifying behavior at runtime.

Enum

Short for "enumeration," an enum in TypeScript is a special data type that enables a variable to hold a set of predefined constants. This feature improves code readability and maintainability.

G

Generic

A powerful feature in TypeScript that allows for creating reusable components by defining a placeholder type that can be replaced with a specific type during implementation.

I

Interface

A TypeScript construct that defines a contract for shapes of objects. It specifies what properties and methods an object must have, facilitating the design of complex data structures with type safety.

Implementation

The process of executing a plan, design, or model. In TypeScript, this refers to the actual coding of classes, functions, or components that adhere to defined interfaces.

J

JavaScript

The core programming language of the web, which TypeScript is built upon. TypeScript is essentially a superset of JavaScript, adding static typing and other features.

M

Module

A way to organize and encapsulate code in TypeScript. Modules can export functions, objects, or classes to be reused in other parts of the application.

O

Object

An instance of a class that can contain properties and methods. In TypeScript, objects can be typed explicitly or flexibly to enforce structure while allowing some level of dynamism.

P

Promise

An object that represents the eventual completion or failure of an asynchronous operation and its resulting value. TypeScript enhances JavaScript promises with type annotations.

Primitive Types

Basic data types that are built into TypeScript, including `number`, `string`, `boolean`, `null`, `undefined`, and `symbol`. They serve as the foundation for more complex data structures.

R

Return Type

The data type of the value that a function returns. Specifying return types in TypeScript helps with clarity and error-checking during development.

S

Static Typing

A feature of TypeScript that allows developers to define the types of variables and function return values, providing compile-time type checking and enhancing code reliability.

TSLint

A static analysis tool used to enforce coding standards and best practices in TypeScript projects. TSLint helps maintain code quality by identifying potential errors early in the development process.

T

Type

A classification of data that determines the operations that can be performed on it. TypeScript enhances JavaScript's dynamic typing with static types to foster better error detection.

Type Inference

A feature of TypeScript where the compiler automatically determines the type of a variable based on its initial value. This minimizes the need for explicit type annotations while providing type safety.

TypeScript

A strongly typed programming language developed by Microsoft, which builds on JavaScript by adding static types. It is increasingly favored for large-scale application development due to its enhanced tooling and maintainability.

U

Union Type

A type that allows a variable to hold one of several types. In TypeScript, this feature allows for flexible function parameters and return types, enhancing code reuse.

V

Variable Declaration

The process of creating a variable in TypeScript using keywords like `let`, `const`, or `var`, along with optional type annotations.

W

Webpack

A powerful static module bundler for modern JavaScript applications, commonly used in TypeScript projects. Webpack helps manage dependencies and compile TypeScript into JavaScript.

www.ingramcontent.com/pod-product-compliance
Lightning Source LLC
Chambersburg PA
CBHW070945050326
40689CB00014B/3351